ANNABEL

52
WAYS TO
TRANSFORM
YOUR LIFE

WEEKLY WISDOM
FOR BUSY PEOPLE

Cover painting by Tim Ivanič.

All those referred to by name in this book
are quoted with their permission

Matador
9 Priory Business Park,
Wistow Road, Kibworth Beauchamp,
Leicestershire. LE8 0RX
Tel: (+44) 116 279 2299
Fax: (+44) 116 279 2277
Email: books@troubador.co.uk
Web: www.troubador.co.uk/matador

ISBN 978 1780881 157

British Library Cataloguing in Publication Data.
A catalogue record for this book is available from the British Library.

Typeset by Troubador Publishing Ltd, Leicester, UK

Matador is an imprint of Troubador Publishing Ltd

Printed in Great Britain by the MPG Books Group, Bodmin and King's Lynn

This book is dedicated to Don,
with my love

For the most wonderful
Annie –
with love,
Annabel Sutta.

Nov. 2012

About This Book

From conversations with clients, colleagues and friends, I know that the one thing everyone is desperately short of is *TIME*. We're rushed off our feet, spinning too many plates and — even though we'd love to make changes in our lives — it's hard to find the space to read and digest the books that can help us.

That's why I wrote *52 Ways to Transform Your Life*. If you're hungry for inspiration and motivation, but strapped for time, it offers fifty-two short Life Coaching Tips that are quick-to-read and easy to put into practice. They're packed full of practical ideas, resources and inspiration to help you to make positive changes in your life.

There's a Tip for each week of the year. Many relate to significant dates in the calendar, so you can choose to start at Tip One (which offers a different perspective on New Year Resolutions) and work your way through to December — or you might prefer to read the whole book in one go — or dip in at random.

Whichever method you choose, each time you pick up the book you'll read something that will help to shape your week — encourage and energize you —and perhaps inspire you to do things differently.

May this book be your catalyst for change!

Annabel

About Annabel Sutton, PCC

Annabel runs a thriving global coaching business and writes regular columns for two papers. She has been coaching since 1999 and was one of the first life coaches in the UK to be awarded a coaching credential. She became a Professional Certified Coach in 2005.

She loves working with unconventional people who want to live and do things differently. Her clients say she's inspiring, energising and fun to work with and she gets great results.

Annabel lived overseas for 15 years (five years in Indonesia and ten in Southern California). She's travelled widely and survived divorce, riots, earthquakes and many career changes. She's learned a lot about life over the years and brings that knowledge and wisdom to her work.

This is her fourth book. Previous titles are:
➢   *The Islands In Between, Travels in Indonesia*
➢   *52 Ways to Handle It*
➢   *52 Ways to Change Your Life*

Annabel lives on the Wiltshire/Dorset border and is passionate about the countryside, good food and organic gardening. Her allotment is symbolic of her life — quirky and a bit non-conformist but surprisingly productive!

For more information about Annabel — about Life Coaching — and to sign up for Annabel's free Coaching Tips visit
www.annabelsutton.com

What Readers Say

What I love about Annabel's tips is that they are always written in a very down to earth way. Because they are short and succinct, I am never too busy to read them. They are relevant, practical and usually very poignant. I often find myself nodding along as I read about her experiences and her tips on how to change things, small or large. Keep them coming!

Marcelle Samuels

I have a shelf full of personal development books that rarely get opened. Annabel's tips are quick to digest, relevant and backed up with real life experience. Most of all they act as a trigger for me to slow down, take stock and begin to address something I've been putting off!

Marie Clement, Elite Edge Marketing Consultants

You know how good it feels to have a warmly supportive hand on your shoulder, guiding you along? Annabel's tips are just like that. Whenever you are hesitating and need a gentle nudge, read one of these tips and you will find you can float more easily through your difficulties and move more confidently forward in your life.

Mary Potter

Always bright, supportive, wise and encouraging. Annabel's Coaching Tips are spot on for helping me make real improvements!

Roseanne Edwards, Journalist

I have enjoyed your coaching tips over the years and have thoroughly appreciated the common sense they often convey.
Ian Rankin, Managing Director, Dot Medical Ltd

Annabel's tips help me get back up when I'm down; they help me to re-focus and have been an inspiration for some of my training courses.
Nicola Elliott, Global IT Training & Competency Manager

I always seem to come across one of Annabel's tips at just the right time. Fantastic for motivation and inspiration.
Dr Karen Janes, Reiki Master/Teacher, Practitioner of The Honey Method

Annabel's tips help to put things back in perspective; they are easy-to-follow and incredibly smart suggestions to help boost self-esteem, productivity, and help you achieve your goals.
Dr Sarah McCormack, Veterinary Surgeon

Contents

About This Book/About Annabel/What Readers Say   iv-vii
Acknowledgements   x

Tip 1   Upside down goal setting   1
Tip 2   Can you tell me what you want?   4
Tip 3   The art of getting it wrong   7
Tip 4   Pause, Listen, Engage!   10
Tip 5   Turn up the volume   13
Tip 6   Resolutions derailed? How to get back on track 16
Tip 7   Sorry seems to be the hardest word   19
Tip 8   What if ...?   22
Tip 9   A change is as good as a rest   25
Tip 10   Slow down and hear the music   28
Tip 11   Create a dream board   31
Tip 12   Feed the need   34
Tip 13   Our Deepest Fear   37
Tip 14   The power of choice   39
Tip 15   Accentuate the positive   42
Tip 16   Springtime energy boost   45
Tip 17   Getting the balance right   48
Tip 18   Procrastination Busting (part one)   51
Tip 19   Procrastination Busting (part two)   54
Tip 20   The power of truth   57
Tip 21   Moi, je ne regrette rien   60
Tip 22   Don't ask *why?*   63
Tip 23   Six steps at a time   66
Tip 24   Trying it on   69
Tip 25   How to stop wasting time and get more done   72
Tip 26   Boost your confidence   75
Tip 27   Getting feedback   78

Tip 28 Pictures at an Exhibition   81
Tip 29 Never ever give up   84
Tip 30 Outrageous goal setting   87
Tip 31 Have you joined the Karma Army?   90
Tip 32 Doing a Scarlett   93
Tip 33 The 80/20 Rule   96
Tip 34 The miracle question   99
Tip 35 Kicking the habit   102
Tip 36 Do yourself differently   105
Tip 37 Pause   108
Tip 38 Develop an optimism habit   110
Tip 39 Unfinished business   113
Tip 40 Three simple goals   116
Tip 41 What's your mantra?   119
Tip 42 The obstacle is the path   122
Tip 43 Follow the energy   125
Tip 44 Living purposefully   127
Tip 45 What would you like to have happen?   130
Tip 46 Extreme self-respect   133
Tip 47 From darkness into light   135
Tip 48 Reasons to be cheerful   138
Tip 49 Fertile void   141
Tip 50 Last words   144
Tip 51 Christmas stress survival kit   147
Tip 52 'Tis the season ... for reflection   150

A note from Annabel   153
References: books and people mentioned   155

Acknowledgements

They say that writing a book is a lonely business and in many ways that's true. But there are many people who have helped and supported me as I've struggled to write and, critically, finish this book.

First and foremost my thanks to Don Hartridge who has read and edited these Tips so many times that I'm surprised we're still speaking. I'm grateful for his careful eye and his ability to rein in my liberal use of adjectives.

As always, I'm hugely grateful to my wonderful family for their love and support. In particular my aunt, Claire Lorrimer, for her help and advice; and my sister Roz Ivanič , who spent many, many hours helping me with various aspects of this book.

Friends have offered invaluable practical and moral support along the way. My special thanks to Judi Goodwin, the late Lynne Walker (who I miss terribly) and to Sue Brown, Pam Drysdale and Joanna Saatchi. Without your support I may well have faltered. Thanks, too, to Annie Lionnet who, on that fateful March day in 2010, gave me the kick up the backside I needed to get started on this book.

Finally, to all those who have shared their experiences and offered help and advice on publishing: Michael Mann, Sarah Sutton, Kul Cuthbert, Jackee Holder, Sharon Eden, Karen Williams, TeeJay Dowe, Mindy Gibbons-Klein, Zoe Meyer and Jen Carter.

The Publishers are grateful to Marianne Williamson for her permission to quote Our Deepest Fear (Tip 13). Also to Alastair Humphreys for his permission to quote Pause (Tip 37). In some instances we have been unable to trace the owners of copyright material and we would appreciate any information that would enable us to do so.

Tip 1: Upside Down Goal Setting

We will open the book. Its pages are blank.
We are going to put words on them ourselves.
The book is called Opportunity and
its first chapter is New Year's Day.
Edith Lovejoy Pierce

I'm not a great fan of New Year Resolutions. Naturally, the dawning of a brand new year is a great time to take stock and think about all the changes we want to make; but experience shows that the majority of resolutions fall by the wayside, and by February most of us will be back to our bad old ways.

So if you want to make changes — and like the idea of doing things a bit differently this year — here's a new approach:

Imagine that it's the end of the year and you're sitting down to reflect on the successes and achievements of the year just passed. Sit down with paper and pen and at the top of the page write *"20_ _ was a great year for me because ..."* Then simply write a list of all the things you've achieved and what it was that made it such a great year.

It may feel a bit strange, but you'll be surprised at how much easier it is to approach things this way. Imagining that your successes have already happened is a great way to set your intentions for the remainder of the year and should leave you feeling inspired, energised and motivated. That's a lot better than the sinking feeling that so often accompanies setting New Year Resolutions.

All you have to do now is plan how you're going to make those achievements happen. Using a year planner, diary or Outlook, make a note of what you need to do and when. Some goals will be straightforward, e.g. *book weekend break in May*. Others may require action on a daily or weekly basis. Break bigger goals down into small action steps and schedule each step.

To help you get started, you can download a handy Goal Planner *(5 Goals to Reach in the Next 90 Days)* from the Free Stuff page on my website.

The future is simply infinite possibility waiting to happen.
What it waits on is human imagination
to crystallize its possibility.
Leland Kaiser

Write it down.
Written goals have a way of transforming
wishes into wants; cant's into cans;
dreams into plans; and plans into reality.
Don't just think it - ink it!
Author Unknown

Tip 2: Can you Tell me What you Want?

*The world makes way for the man who knows
where he is going.*
Ralph Waldo Emerson

The start of the year is traditionally a time when we turn our thoughts to making changes in our lives. And at the heart of this process lies the most fundamental of questions: What do I want — what do I *really* want?

It's surprising how many people find this question so hard to answer. It's often clouded by what they think they *ought* to want — or what other people tell them they *should* want. Or perhaps the vision of what they would really love to do has become obscured by doubt, fear and insecurity. As a result they've lost track of what would make them feel happy, fulfilled and productive.

The truth is that it's often much easier to identify what we *don't* want. For example, let's say you're finding it difficult to clarify what kind of job you'd enjoy and would find fulfilling. I'd bet that if I asked you to tell me all the things you *didn't* want you'd be able to give me an exhaustive list.

So here's an exercise to try. Using the same example, write a detailed description of your *Job from Hell*. Outline all the aspects of a job that you know you wouldn't want, or that would make you thoroughly miserable. Then simply flip the items on your list over to get an indication of what would make you happy.

Once you've identified *what* you want you can start to make your plans for the year.

All of us were meant to be happy and successful.
Life is more than a two-week vacation once a year.
It is, and can be, exactly what you want it to be.
There are no limits except those you put on yourself.
Thomas D Willhite

When you determine what you want,
you have made the most important decision in your life.
You have to know what you want in order to attain it.
Douglas Lurtan

Tip 3: The Art of Getting it Wrong

Mistakes are the portals of discovery.
James Joyce

When was the last time you watched a small child learning to walk? They'll take a couple of steps, fall over, pick themselves up and try again. Heaven knows how many times they fall over before they master the art of walking. They might cry the first time they fall down — they might be a bit surprised and perplexed — but do they give up? No. There isn't the tiniest question of giving up and they get back on their feet and try again.

Just imagine, if a child stopped and thought too much about walking, he or she would probably never start. They could spend days, weeks, months thinking about it and preparing for it, taking umpteen courses and reading books on *how to walk* but never actually do it. Perfectionists and procrastinators can learn a lot from toddlers. Not only do they put off doing things, but sometimes they're so paralysed by the fear of not getting it right that they shelve an idea completely. They over-think and over-prepare, worried that they'll never know enough or be good enough.

Successful entrepreneurs and toddlers have a lot in common. They're both risk takers and refuse to give up. Entrepreneurs typically don't become successful overnight. In fact, they may suffer several disastrous failures before they experience success.

So what can we learn from this? Maybe to overcome the curse of perfectionism we have to return to child-like thinking. Don't prepare. Don't think or analyse. Just do it. Be prepared to fall over, pick yourself up, fall over again. Enjoy the process, rather than worry about the outcome. You may not get it right the first time, or even the second — but with persistence you'll make it in the end.

Several years ago I was struggling with writing the text for my first website and kept putting it off because I felt I had to do it 'right'. I was on the verge of giving up when I read a newsletter by US marketing expert, Robert Middleton, on exactly this topic. He recalled how, many years before, he had struggled with his first website. It wasn't perfect — in fact, the look and feel of the site has changed several times since that first effort. He has, effectively, fallen over many times before eventually fashioning the product he wanted. The point was that he had made a start and done *something*.

Accepting that what you do actually doesn't have to be perfect first time has helped me a lot over the years. It can be changed. It probably WILL be changed. Sometimes you just have to recognise that what you undertake probably won't be perfect. But you can always strive for 80% *(see Tip 33: The 80/20 Rule)*. We will do the very best we can, at the time, and with the resources available to us. The important thing is to get started.

QUESTION: *Have you made enough mistakes recently?*

Perfectionism has nothing to do with getting it right.
It has nothing to do with fixing things.
It has nothing to do with standards.
Perfectionism is a refusal to let yourself move ahead.
Julia Cameron

Anyone who has never made a mistake has never
tried anything new.
Albert Einstein

Tip 4: Pause, Listen, Engage!

Yes and No are very short words to say,
but we should think for some length of time
before saying them.
Author Unknown

Inspired, no doubt, by the referee's instructions to players before a rugby scrum to 'crouch, touch, pause, engage' — in April 2011 the Coalition Government announced their intention to 'Pause, Listen and Engage' in order to consider all sides of the argument regarding their proposed Health and Social Care bill.

It struck me that this would be a brilliant 3-Step Strategy for all those times when we need to say *"No"*.

Here's how it works.

Step One: When you receive a request to do or get involved in something the first thing to do is to PAUSE. Instead of automatically saying "yes", find a way to put some space between the request and your response. This could be as simple as saying you'll get back to them in an hour, or let them know tomorrow or next week. It's really important to give yourself some thinking space.

Step Two: The next step is to LISTEN ... to yourself. Is this something you genuinely want to do? Or is it something you feel you should do? Can you say yes to it wholeheartedly?

By saying yes to this, what else in your life are you saying no to? How will this additional activity affect your life balance? What about your down time? Does it fit with your overall plan for the year? Does it accord with your values and what's really important to you?

Step Three: Only when you've Paused and Listened can you then choose to ENGAGE — or not.

*Half of the troubles of this life can be traced to
saying yes too quickly
and not saying no soon enough.*
Josh Billings

*Now and then it's good to pause
in our pursuit of happiness
and just be happy.*
Guillaume Apollinaire

Tip 5: Turn up the Volume

Learn to get in touch with the silence within yourself and know that everything in this life has a purpose.
Elisabeth Kubler-Ross

Some years ago one of my clients used an intriguing metaphor to describe what was happening to him. He explained that he kept hearing a certain message about what he should do next in his life. Because the message referred to a pretty radical life change — not something he wanted to take on board at the time — he kept trying to ignore it. He kept 'turning down the volume' (as you would on a radio) so that he couldn't hear it any longer. But, no matter how hard he tried to ignore it, as the months went by the message kept coming back — getting louder and louder until he couldn't ignore it any longer.

Have you ever had a similar experience? Are there messages right now that are trying to break through the static? Do you keep turning down the volume because it's too scary or uncomfortable to think about them? Or perhaps you haven't given yourself permission to explore the possibilities inherent in them?

While many of us use logic to make decisions and set our life course, I believe that it's really important to listen to our intuition as well. There are certainly times in my life when I've chosen to turn down the volume and have later regretted that I didn't listen more carefully.

In the relentlessly noisy world we live in it can be tough to quieten down enough to let the messages filter through. So you might have to take conscious steps to make space in your life for reflection. Many people find that meditation helps them to still the mind. In her book 'The Artist's Way' Julia Cameron recommends writing a stream of consciousness first thing every morning. Perhaps taking a walk on your own — or making time to sit quietly — I know someone who does his best thinking when he's out running... whatever works for you.

So, my tip for this week is to keep your eyes and ears open. Listen and look for the messages. Turn up the volume and listen to your own wisdom. Most importantly, when you get an intuitive hit, pay attention to it even if it feels uncomfortable. Give yourself permission to consider all the possibilities. Who knows where they might take you?

Every time you don't follow your inner guidance,
you feel a loss of energy,
loss of power, a sense of spiritual deadness.
Shakti Gawain

Like an ability or a muscle, hearing your inner wisdom
is strengthened by doing it.
Robbie Gass

Tip 6: Resolutions Derailed? How to Get Back on Track

Try not. Do, or do not. There is no try.
Yoda, the Jedi Master

Experience shows that, despite our best intentions, by the time we get to February most of our New Year Resolutions will have fallen by the wayside. If your resolve has started to falter, here are a few ideas to help you get back on track.

Make an Action Plan
Get your goals out of your head and onto paper. Ideally, translate them into a clear Action Plan with timelines and deadlines. Do you need to cut your goals down into smaller steps? If so, are there actions you need to take on a daily, weekly or monthly basis?

Make yourself accountable
Accountability is the enemy of inactivity. Making yourself accountable for your progress can make a huge difference to your success. Some clients send me their Action Plan at the start of each month and then send daily or weekly updates to help them stay focused. Do you know someone you could do this with?

Anticipate obstacles
Even armed with loads of enthusiasm and goals that inspire us, we can still encounter obstacles. What could get in the way of you achieving your goals this year? What are your

personal stumbling blocks? Procrastination? Perfectionism? Taking on too much and not being able to say 'no'? Fear? Lack of confidence? Think about the lessons you've learned from previous years and see if you can come up with a contingency plan you can put into action the moment you find yourself faltering.

Get some support

Gather a good support team around you. Whether it's your family, friends, work colleagues, boss or coach, having someone to keep you on track — cheer you on, celebrate your successes and pick you up and dust you off when you falter — is really important. Group support can be particularly effective: how about getting together a small group of friends or colleagues who can support each other?

Bolster your self-belief

This is a tricky one. How to deal with the Inner Critic who has such a knack of popping up when least wanted and derailing us by scuppering our self-confidence? Again, enlisting others to support you can really help. Another idea is to create a 'Feel Good' Box for those days when your confidence is waning (see Tip 26: Boost Your Confidence).

Most importantly, if you have a bad day, don't beat yourself up — pick yourself up and start afresh tomorrow.

The secret of success is constancy of purpose.
Benjamin Disraeli

Let me tell you the secret that has led to my goal.
My strength lies solely in my tenacity.
Louis Pasteur

Our greatest weakness lies in giving up.
The most certain way to succeed is to always try,
just one more time.
Thomas Edison

Tip 7: Sorry Seems to be the Hardest Word

An apology is the superglue of life.
It can repair just about anything.
Lynn Johnston

Why are the words *'I'm sorry'* so hard to say? Is it because we're admitting that we've failed or done something 'wrong'? Is it because it shines a light on our weakness and vulnerability? Does it just feel a whole lot easier to shift the blame onto someone or something else instead?

Some years ago I delivered a workshop with a colleague at a London hotel. At the end of the day we went to Reception to pay and were presented with a considerably larger bill than we had expected. This was *not* what we wanted to hear.

The Manager was summoned and he quickly summed up the situation. His reaction was swift. He acknowledged that there had been an error, apologised for the mistake and asked if we would like to sit in the bar and enjoy a bottle of champagne on the house while he sorted out the problem. Naturally, we were pleasantly surprised, accepted the offer, and spent the next ten minutes extolling the virtues of the hotel. Not only that, but in the following weeks we both sold the hotel to others as a training venue. The manager had succeeded in turning a potentially disastrous situation into a positive one, turning us from complaining customers to complimentary clients.

For those of us who run our own businesses, we don't have to panic if we make a mistake — in fact it can be a gift if we act in the right way. Just follow the same steps as the Hotel Manager: 1) Acknowledge the mistake 2) Apologise 3) Go out of your way to put it right. If you really pull the stops out to right the wrong, people will tell others *not* about the mistake but about the superb and imaginative way in which you handled it.

Exactly the same principle applies in our personal lives. If we've done something to upset someone else (or vice versa) and we refuse to acknowledge it or apologise, the issue hangs around and never seems to get resolved. But if we take full responsibility for our mistake, apologise and go out of our way to repair the wrong, everyone benefits. The upset is forgotten, resentment evaporates and happiness is restored.

So in this Valentine's week my challenge to you is this: if you've made a mistake of any kind, admit it, apologise and make amends for it. Those around you — particularly your nearest and dearest — will love you more for doing so.

*It is the highest form of self-respect to admit our errors
and mistakes and make amends for them.
To make a mistake is only an error in judgment,
but to adhere to it when it is discovered
shows infirmity of character.*
Dale E. Turner

*People spend too much time finding other people to blame,
too much energy finding excuses for not being
what they are capable of being, and not enough
energy putting themselves on the line, growing out of
the past and getting on with their lives.*
J. Michael Straczynski

Tip 8: What If...?

It's kind of fun to do the impossible!
Walt Disney

What If questions can lead you to exciting places. They open up doors and take you into the realm of the possible.

When working with groups I'll often use Roger von Oech's Creative Whack Pack. This is a pack of cards designed to *whack* you out of habitual thought patterns and allow you to look at what you're doing in a fresh way. At a recent group coaching session I dealt five cards to each person and everyone had the opportunity to relate one or more of their cards to their life.

The card that generated the most discussion and which, ultimately, had the greatest impact on the group was the one entitled *ASK WHAT IF?* The card reads: *Put some magic in your thinking by asking 'what if' questions. What if animals became more intelligent than people? What if we had mouths in the palms of our hands? What if we had edible clothing? Such questions will stretch your thinking and lead to new ideas...*

The key question that emerged from our coaching session, and which really got everybody thinking, was *What if I didn't care what anyone else thought?*

Such a simple question, but with such profound implications.

It invites a radical shift towards living a life on your own terms and without the constraint of living up to the expectations of others. Clearly, unless you're a hermit you will need to take account of those who live with and around you, but in its broader context this question is truly liberating.

Here are a few more to consider:

➢ *What if I knew I couldn't fail?*
➢ *What if I didn't have to do it perfectly?*
➢ *What if I wasn't afraid?*
➢ *What if I really believed in myself?*
➢ *What if anything was possible?*

Embrace the possibilities and have a great week.

The potential of the average person is like
a huge ocean unsailed,
a new continent unexplored,
a world of possibilities waiting to be released and
channelled toward some great good.
Brian Tracy

Even a thought, even a possibility,
can shatter and transform us.
Friedrich Nietzsche

Anyone honest will tell you that possibility is far
more frightening than impossibility.
Julia Cameron

Tip 9: A Change is as Good as a Rest

Take rest; a field that has rested gives a bountiful crop.
Ovid

The midst of winter is a time when many people complain of feeling weary and run down. When we feel this way, it's tempting to want to stay at home, hunker down and sleep more — whereas research has shown that the most invigorating thing we can do at this time of year is not to sleep more, but to take ourselves out of our normal routine and do something totally different.

I really do believe in the value of disrupting our routine and doing something new as a way to refresh and energise ourselves. According to research by Ebookers published in the Metro newspaper, more than a quarter of Britons make life-changing decisions while away and a large percentage find their trips inspirational. Apparently, 15% split up with their partner, 10% decide to start a family and another 10% propose. 10% decide to move abroad, 12% want a career change and 30% will learn a new skill.

We all know that holidays refresh us, but you don't necessarily have to go away for a week or fly to a foreign country to get the same benefits. A day or weekend away can work wonders — as can going on a stimulating course or workshop; visiting a gallery; going to a new place; trying a new sport or hobby ... the possibilities are endless.

At the beginning of every year, my client Lin makes a commitment to do something in the coming year that she's never done before. She says that it takes her out of her normal routine, shakes things up a bit and gives her something to look forward to. Past experiences have included going for a ride in a hot-air balloon, zip-wiring over the rain forest, and racing in a yacht (having never sailed before). Some of these involve overseas travel and a generous budget, but there's no reason why you can't follow a similar path (closer to home and on a smaller budget) and get the same benefits.

Simply getting away from your normal environment can be stimulating. Getting out of the house or office and going for a walk in the country, sitting in the buzz and energy of a bustling café or walking round an art gallery can do wonders for sparking new ideas and connections.

As we shake off the darkness of winter and turn towards spring, there's no better time to plan things that are new and stimulating and, crucially, get you away from your normal routine — you'll feel so much better for it.

QUESTION: What might you do this year that you've never done before?

Measurement of life should be proportioned rather to the intensity of the experience than to its actual length.
Thomas Hardy

Change is the law of life.
And those who look only to the past or the present are certain to miss the future.
John F. Kennedy

You cannot step twice into the same river, for other waters are continually flowing in.
Heraclitus

Tip 10: Slow Down and Hear the Music

People in a hurry cannot think, cannot grow,
nor can they decay.
They are preserved in a state of perpetual puerility.
Eric Hoffer

Washington DC Metro Station on a cold January morning in 2007...

A man with a violin played six Bach pieces for about an hour. During that time approximately two thousand people walked through the station, most of them on their way to work. After three minutes a middle-aged man noticed there was a musician playing. He slowed down, stopped for a few seconds and then hurried on.

30 seconds later: The violinist received his first dollar: a woman threw the money in the hat and continued walking.

After 6 minutes: A young man leaned against the wall to listen, then glanced at his watch and walked away.

After 10 minutes: A 3-year old boy stopped but his mother tugged him along impatiently. The child stopped to look at the violinist again, but was pulled away by his mother. The child walked on reluctantly, turning back to look at the musician with every step. Several other children stopped but every parent, without exception, forced them to move on.

After 45 minutes: The musician had played continuously. During that time only six people stopped and listened for a short while. Twenty gave money but continued to walk on. The man had collected a total of $32.

After 1 hour: He finished playing. No one noticed. No one applauded. And the sounds of the station took over.

The violinist was Joshua Bell, one of the world's greatest musicians. He had played some of the most intricate Bach pieces ever written, on a violin worth $3.5 million. Two days beforehand Bell had sold out a concert hall in Boston where the seats averaged $100.

This is a true story. The Washington Post invited Joshua Bell to play incognito in the metro station as part of a social experiment about perception, taste and people's priorities. The questions raised: in a common-place environment at an inappropriate hour, do we perceive beauty? Do we stop to appreciate it? Do we recognise talent in an unexpected context?

If we don't have a moment to stop and listen to one of the best musicians in the world, playing some of the finest music ever written, with one of the most beautiful instruments ever made... how many other things are we missing?

What is this life if, full of care,
we have no time to stand and stare?
W.H. Davies

Hurry, hurry has no blessing.
Swahili Proverb

If there is to be any peace it will come
through being, not having.
Henry Miller

Tip 11: Create a Dream Board

*Too many of us are not living our dreams
because we are living our fears.*
Les Brown

There's little point working hard on clarifying our goals and vision for the future only to file it all away neatly — out of sight out of mind. A *Dream (or Vision) Board* is a visual representation of your goals and is a great way to keep your vision fresh and active. You can see the exciting future you're working towards at a glance, and this will help keep you motivated and on track.

Your Dream Board can contain images, colours, words, poems, song lyrics, symbols, drawings — anything that you feel represents your vision in some way. I've seen a rather enigmatic picture of three plates on a Dream Board because their pastel shades represented a particular sense of calm and serenity for its creator. It doesn't have to make sense to anyone but you.

Alissa, one of my clients, leaves a few spots empty on her board so that she can edit her dreams and add new ones. She explains, *"In this way, the Dream Board is constantly evolving and doesn't just become a piece of furniture in my room that I don't take notice of. More of an interactive thing, which totally helps with my day-to-day motivation."*

Once your Dream Board is finished put it somewhere where you'll see it on a regular basis and use it as a visual reminder of your goals and dreams. Keep asking yourself, as Alissa does, *"What can I do today to help me achieve those dreams?"*

Think BIG.
There are unseen forces ready to support your dreams.
Cheryl Richardson

As soon as you start to pursue a dream,
your life wakes up and everything has meaning.
Barbara Sher

Tip 12: Feed the Need

Understanding human needs is half
the job of meeting them.
Adlai Stevenson

When I was a child I went to my cousin's birthday party. A magician had been booked to entertain us and at the end of his act he invited my cousin onto the stage to help him perform the final trick. When I got home I begged my mother to let me have the same magician at my birthday party — not because I liked his tricks, but because I wanted to be the one he invited up on stage to help him.

He did, indeed, perform at my party and I could hardly wait for him to ask me to help him with his last trick. But when the moment finally arrived he chose someone else and I was absolutely devastated.

Why do I tell this story? Because incidents like these can be a goldmine for understanding our emotional needs. This story shows me that I had (and indeed still have) a need to be the centre of attention.

Being aware of our emotional needs, and making sure they're met, is one of the foundation stones of a fulfilled life. Clearly, we all have basic physical needs (for food, water, shelter, warmth). But what about our emotional needs? We all have these, too, and they will vary from person to person. To love/feel loved, to be appreciated, to feel respected, to be independent, to feel secure, to feel needed, to feel protected, to be in control and so on.

Emotional needs are incredibly powerful and they can drive our behaviour and choices in ways we may not even be aware of. And this is where they can be dangerous. For example, a need to be right can get you into all sorts of trouble in your relationships; while a need to be 'top dog' could cause you to make ill-advised business decisions.

So how do we find out what our emotional needs are? A strong indicator is if we find ourselves becoming irrationally angry or upset about something. Let's say you're having a conversation with someone and they consistently fail to acknowledge what you're saying. As the conversation continues you notice that you're becoming more and more upset. When something like this happens, check for the emotional need lurking underneath. In this case, it could be that you have a need to be heard or acknowledged and this need is being trampled on.

Once you know what your needs are you can take steps to make sure they're being met in healthy ways. For example, if you have a need to be appreciated, this could make life at work very difficult if your boss or line manager never express any appreciation for your hard work. So see if you can find a way to let them know that you'd really appreciate some positive feedback.

Making yourself vulnerable enough to ask someone to meet one of your needs isn't easy, but the payoff is often tremendous for both parties.

Everybody needs beauty as well as bread,
places to play in and pray in
where nature may heal and cheer
and give strength to the body and soul.
John Muir

We all have different desires and needs,
but if we don't discover what we want from ourselves
and what we stand for, we will live
passively and unfulfilled.
Bill Watterson

They say a person needs just three things to be truly happy
in this world: someone to love, something to do and
something to hope for.
Tom Bodett

Tip 13: Our Deepest Fear

Our deepest fear is not that we are inadequate.

Our deepest fear is that we are powerful beyond measure.

It is our light, not our darkness that most frightens us.

We ask ourselves,

Who am I to be brilliant, gorgeous, talented, fabulous?

Actually, who are you <u>not</u> to be?

You are a child of God.

Your playing small does not serve the world.

There's nothing enlightened about shrinking so that other people won't feel insecure around you.

We are all meant to shine, as children do.

We were born to make manifest the glory of God that is within us.

It's not just in some of us; it's in everyone.

And as we let our own light shine,

we unconsciously give other people permission to do the same.

As we are liberated from our own fear,

our presence automatically liberates others.

Marianne Williamson, A Return To Love

It is your mind that creates the world.
The Buddha

If you cannot be a poet, be the poem.
David Carradine

*If you hear a voice within you saying 'you are not a painter',
then by all means paint ...
and that voice will be silenced.*
Vincent van Gogh

Tip 14: The Power of Choice

Destiny is not a matter of chance, it is a matter of choice;
it is not a thing to be waited for,
it is a thing to be achieved.
William Jennings Bryan

There was a really interesting programme on TV a few years ago about the different choices people make in response to similar events. It highlighted two sets of parents who had lost their daughters in the downing of Pan Am flight 103 at Lockerbie. Same dreadful incident — same tragic loss — and yet they had chosen very different responses. One set of parents had put all their energy into grappling with the legal system and canvassing the US government to bring the bomber to justice, while the others had set up a charitable foundation in their daughter's memory to help other bereaved families. The difference in demeanour between the two couples was quite startling: the first appeared consumed with bitterness and the quest for revenge, while the second seemed to have found some sort of peace by channelling their grief into something they felt was worthwhile.

At times when events and life feel overwhelming — when negativity threatens to take over — it can be very reassuring to remind ourselves that each one of us ultimately possesses the power of choice. It's a well-known maxim, for example, that while we have no power over the way others behave towards us, we have absolute power of choice over the way we react.

Coach Michael Neill has a great take on this. He suggests that whenever we find ourselves caught up in negative thinking, we apply the concept of a 'train of thought' literally. In other words, if you find yourself spiralling into negative thinking (a negative train of thought) simply choose to get off the train. Trains go in lots of different directions... if you don't like where your train of thought is heading, choose to get off and find one that's going in a more positive direction.

It's so simple — and so clever. The power of choice. Just get off the train.

Whenever I have to choose between two evils, I always like to try the one I haven't tried before.
Mae West

How you choose to respond each moment to the movie of life determines how you see the next frame, and the next, and eventually how you feel when the movie ends.
Doc Childre

Tip 15: Accentuate the Positive

Success is achieved by developing our strengths,
not by eliminating our weaknesses.
Marilyn vos Savant

I'm a great fan of Positive Psychology. One of its principles is that if we focus on our strengths rather than our weaknesses — and when we're able to honour our innate strengths in our personal and professional lives — we'll all be a lot happier.

You may think this sounds obvious, but out in the real world it's often more common for people to pick up on other people's weaknesses and criticise them rather than encourage their strengths. Come to think of it, how often do we beat *ourselves* up for not doing something well enough rather than patting ourselves on the back for doing a great job?

Here are some ways that Positive Psychology principles can be applied to our day-to-day lives:

The Strength Story
Think of a time when you were at your best. Where were you? What were you doing? What strengths were you demonstrating? Recall this experience in as much detail as you can. You could write it down and keep it (perhaps re-read it if you're having an off day), or illustrate it and pin it up somewhere — maybe on your Dream Board (see Tip 11), or your Feel Good Box (see Tip 26). If you have children, could you use this with them?

Focus on your strengths
What would you say are your top five strengths? Choose one and use it as your 'theme for the week'. If you encounter a problem or challenge, or if you have a tough decision to make, draw on that strength to help you handle it.

360 degree positive feedback
This is my favourite. Apparently at the Positive Psychology offices they hold regular feedback sessions where each person is given positive feedback by everyone in the room. Amongst other things they're told what everyone appreciates about them and what they've done really well in the last week. Just imagine what it would be like if this was done in offices all over the country? Wouldn't it be great? What would the effect be if we used positive feedback regularly at home as well?

I appreciate that life can't always be as relentlessly upbeat as this, and that there is a place for constructive criticism, but I'm a firm believer in how much happier we'd be if we made a conscious effort to focus on our own, and others' strengths rather than draw attention to their weaknesses.

QUESTION: How can you play to your strengths this week?

If human beings are perceived as potentials rather than problems, as possessing strengths instead of weaknesses, as unlimited rather than dull and unresponsive, then they thrive and grow to their capabilities.
Barbara Bush

We should seek a system that provides outlets for those skills and talents so that everyone can find a way to work and serve in a manner that best suits the strengths of each individual.
Lee R. Raymond

Tip 16: Springtime Energy Boost

The world's favorite season is the Spring.
All things seem possible in May.
Edwin Way Teale

Back in January I bought a one-litre pot of red paint as I wanted to paint one of the walls in my office. Because I didn't get round to the task right away I dumped the pot in the box room and ever since then not only have I tripped over it countless times, but its very presence has acted as a reproach and reminder that the job was still waiting to be done. Every time I looked at it my heart would sink and I'd experience an immediate dip in energy.

Last week I marched purposefully into the box room, opened the pot and painted the wall. It looks great, but more importantly, finally dealing with the thing that's been bugging me for so long resulted in a surge of positive energy.

With the disappearance of winter and the longer days, the coming of spring is a perfect time to give yourself a natural energy boost by dealing with all those things that have been irritating you.

Often it's the tiny things that annoy the most and that are easiest to sort out, such as the dripping tap in the kitchen, that stain on the carpet, a cluttered closet, or the pile of stuff that's waiting to be taken to the tip. At the other end of the spectrum there may be things which will require more time and effort. Perhaps it's your job or a relationship that's getting you down; or you don't like where you live and need to consider moving.

The key is that everything you're tolerating — large and small — will be draining your energy, making you feel irritable and wearing you down. Not only that, but it can reduce your natural ability to attract success. Eliminating these things is one of the key factors underpinning a successful and fulfilling life.

So, make a list of absolutely everything that's annoying you; frustrating you; all the things that you're putting up with. Then start working through it, crossing off each item as you complete it. Start with the easy stuff — this will clear the way and give you the energy you need to face the larger items. Aim to pick at least three and tackle them in the next week. Or you could set aside one whole day, or a weekend, and really blitz the list.

Keep working your way through the list until all the items have been eliminated. Not only will it free up lots of energy but you'll create the space for positive things to come into your life.

When old words die out on the tongue,
new melodies break forth from the heart;
and where the old tracks are lost,
new country is revealed with its wonders.
Rabindranath Tagore

Eliminate something superfluous from your life.
Break a habit.
Do something that makes you feel insecure.
Piero Ferrucci

Tip 17: Getting the Balance Right

And in the end, it's not the years in your life that count.
It's the life in your years.
Abraham Lincoln

Everyone talks about *Work Life Balance* — how important it is — how we all need it. It's become the modern-day Nirvana which we're all striving desperately to achieve.

But what does Work Life Balance actually mean? My guess is that there is no one, definitive answer. In reality, it's likely to mean different things to different people. In a way, the term makes very little sense as work is, for most of us, very much part of our lives. Maybe the term Work/Play or Work/Rest would be more accurate.

The first step to taking control and regaining some balance in our lives is to be clear about what we're actually aiming for. So, what does Work Life Balance mean to you? Jot down a few ideas. Don't worry at this stage if it seems possible or not — just aim to be clear about what, in an ideal world, a balanced life would look and feel like. Once you're clear about what you're aiming for, you could write a description of your ideal balanced week or month.

Another approach is to draw a circle and create a pie chart which illustrates the percentages (be honest) of time currently taken up by all the different areas of your life: Work, Family, Leisure, Sport, Relationship, Me-Time, Hobbies, etc. Is this how you want your life to look?

Now draw the circle again, but this time with your ideal percentage split. What would have to change to make this happen?

Recently, a Sunday paper featured the story of a man who had made drastic changes to restore balance in his life. He'd given up a stratospheric income as a corporate lawyer (with the stress and pressures on his time that corporate life demands) to take a job as an in-house lawyer with a children's charity. His pay quartered, but he said it had transformed his life: he's now much happier and has more time and energy to spend with his family.

Are you ready to do something similar? Or would a couple of smaller steps make a big difference? My challenge to you this week is to do at least one thing that will help to restore the balance of your life. It could be something as simple as doing your grocery shopping online rather than going to the store yourself.

Take a look at the description you've written of your ideal week/month. Consider what could be possible in terms of taking the steps towards making it a reality. Is there anything you need to let go of? The important thing is to do *something*.

*There can be no high civilization where there
is not ample leisure.*
Henry Ward Beecher

*It is balance; we need it. The sad part is that some people
pay more attention to their credit than
they do to their own balance in life!*
Catherine Pulsifer

Tip 18: Procrastination Busting (Part one)

If you want to make an easy job seem mighty hard,
just keep putting off doing it.
Olin Miller

Procrastination is something I know a lot about. As a serial procrastinator I'll find almost anything to do as a diversionary tactic from the task I know I *should* be doing. It's amazing how many trivial jobs just have to be done when I'm faced with a gnarly project or challenging task.

So why do we procrastinate and how can we overcome it? In this, and the following Tip, I offer some suggestions.

Fear
There's almost always some element of fear underlying the tendency to procrastinate. Fear of failure (or success); fear of not doing something well enough (perfectionists will recognise this); fear of being exposed... Fear is an instinctive reaction which is designed to make us get as far away from the cause of the fear as possible — no wonder we'll do anything to avoid the activity associated with it.

Understanding what the fear is all about will make it easier to address. On a sheet of paper, write the words *'I'm afraid of ...'* and complete the sentence as many times as you can. Don't think too hard about it — write the first things that come to mind. Or perhaps you could discuss it with someone objective who can help you think it through. When you're clearer about what the fear is, then you can find creative ways to address it. Do you need to challenge your beliefs and think differently? Find out more information? Get some help, advice or support?

Lack of knowledge, skills, understanding
Sometimes we put off doing things because of a gap in our knowledge or skills. We simply don't know enough to approach the task. In this case, ask yourself *What's missing? Where are the gaps? What do I need to find out? Where could I get this information? Is there someone with the expertise I lack who could give me advice or support? Do I need some specialist training? Do I need to delegate all or part of this to someone else?*

Feeling overwhelmed
Another reason for procrastination is because a task feels too overwhelming. It's a bit of a cliché, but it really does help to break a large project or task down into small, manageable steps. Writing a book feels like a huge mountain to climb, but if you break it down into chapters and then set yourself a goal of writing, say, two pages a day it feels more achievable.

Understanding procrastination takes us one big step closer to getting to grips with it. Tip 19 expands on this further. In the meantime, grab that task, take a deep breath and get started.

*Nothing is so fatiguing as the eternal hanging on
of an uncompleted task.*
William James

*Procrastination is one of the most common and deadliest of
diseases and its toll on success and happiness is heavy.*
Wayne Gretzky

*Procrastination usually results in sorrowful regret.
Today's duties put off until tomorrow give us a
double burden to bear; the best way is to do them
in their proper time.*
Ida Scott Taylor

Tip 19: Procrastination Busting (Part 2)

It's the job that's never started as takes
the longest to finish.
J.R.R. Tolkien

Following on from Tip 18 here are some more reasons why we procrastinate and some tips to help overcome the problem.

You don't enjoy / aren't good at the task
Let's face it, there are some tasks that we aren't naturally good at and don't enjoy. I know many self-employed people who are brilliant at what they do but loathe picking up the phone to speak to prospective customers, and consequently put it off as long as they can. If this is the case, is there someone you could delegate the task to? Somewhere out there is a person who loves doing the thing you detest. Perhaps you could do a skills swap with someone who would find the job easy and enjoy doing it.

Inability to get started
Getting started is the hardest thing for procrastinators. My favourite remedy is coach Mark Forster's strategy of 'just getting the file out.' Having reassured yourself that you don't actually have to DO the task at hand, ask yourself ... *if I were going to do it, what's the **very first thing** I'd have to do to get started?* This might be to simply get the file out.

It could be to switch on the computer; find the phone number of the person you need to call; sit down at a table with a pad of paper, pick up the book ... More often than not you will end up doing that first thing and, having done that, you'll probably get stuck into the task. Just taking that first step is the key.

Everyone knows the procrastination rules: you should set your priorities; you should do the task first before you do anything else, and so on... But you need lots of self-discipline for that, and in my experience that often doesn't work.

So what's the answer? One of the best ways to beat procrastination is to make yourself accountable to someone else. Whether it's a friend or family member, your boss or your coach, making a firm commitment to someone else will make a huge difference to your actually knuckling down and doing it.

So, try making yourself accountable to someone for those task(s) you've been putting off. Perhaps you could 'buddy up' with someone else: make a commitment to each other, agree a deadline and check in with each other to make sure the job is done. It really does work.

For some extra-accountability, check out my Procrastination Buster Days (details on my website) where you can make yourself accountable to a group of others and spend a day in good company, having fun and getting loads of stuff done.

Between saying and doing many a pair of shoes is worn out.
Italian Proverb

There are a million ways to lose a workday,
but not even a single way to get one back.
Tom DeMarco & Timothy Lister

To think too long about doing a thing often
becomes its undoing.
Eva Young

Tip 20: The Power of Truth

Integrity is telling myself the truth.
And honesty is telling the truth to other people.
Spencer Johnson

There was a programme on TV some years ago which followed the trials and tribulations of the inhabitants of a remote village in the Borneo rainforest. A long-running dispute had resulted in considerable hostility between different factions within the village. Their approach to finding a resolution was fascinating: everybody was invited to gather for a communal discussion, and at this meeting each person was asked to 'speak their truth' about the dispute. And so they did. No holds barred — just complete honesty. There were no violent outbursts or recrimination; each person simply explained their point of view and everybody else listened respectfully. The outcome was amazing. Everybody understood everybody else's point of view, months of bitterness and resentment evaporated, a solution was agreed and harmony was restored.

In relationships, where tensions and misunderstandings have built up over a period of time, it's only when both parties sit down and talk things over and really tell their truth (believe me, you *know* when you hear the real truth and not a fabrication or half-truth) that the situation stands a chance of being resolved.

In the same way, I've noticed that when people make decisions which are based on complete honesty about their situation, something extraordinary happens, synchronicity kicks in and things fall into place.

Sometimes it's nothing short of terrifying to speak your truth (as much to yourself as to anyone else), but I'm coming to believe wholeheartedly that when you overcome the fear or the resistance and tell the truth about your life, that you will instantly know it's right; you'll experience a huge sense of relief; you'll feel energised and everything will seem to slot into place.

QUESTION: Is there a truth that you are avoiding? Is there a truth that you need to speak?

We know the truth, not only by the reason,
but also by the heart.
Pascal

Honesty has a beautiful and refreshing simplicity about it.
No ulterior motives. No hidden meanings….
As honesty and real integrity characterize our lives,
there will be no need to manipulate others.
Chuck Swindoll

The house of delusions is cheap to build
but drafty to live in.
A.E. Houseman

Tip 21: Moi, Je Ne Regrette Rien

Whatever you think you can do or believe you can do,
begin it.
Action has magic, grace and power in it.
Goethe

Imagine it's your 80th birthday. You're waking up and feeling excited about the day to come. Where are you? What can you hear? What can you see? It's a special occasion and all your family and friends will be arriving to celebrate the day with you. As you lie in bed you think back over your life and everything you've done up to now... all your experiences ... your work ... your relationships ... your hobbies ... the people you've known. Looking back from this viewpoint, on this day, is there anything you regret NOT having done?

Sometimes when I give talks I'll invite the audience to close their eyes and imagine this scenario. Ideally, of course, we'll reach the age of 80, happy in the knowledge that we've done all the things — large and small — that we really wanted to do. But sadly, this isn't always the case.

Sheila attended one of my talks several years ago and her story beautifully illustrates how this exercise can impact your life. Having done the visualisation she decided to make one of her life-long dreams a reality. She explains: *'One of the things you said when I first met you really struck home with me. It was when we closed our eyes at age 80 and thought back on all the experiences we had had, and all the things we wished we had done.*

So much so that I have made a rather crazy decision, based on an idea that I have harboured deep in my soul for many years. In March I will be setting off to Tibet and will trek to base camp at Everest... just seeing it written down seems to make it even more real! So after March I can close my eyes and always see Everest. Wow that really excites me.'

What an inspiration. And a real life example of someone who had the guts to really push the boundaries to achieve something she felt passionately about. Sheila did achieve her dream to get to Everest Base Camp and has since been back to Annapurna Base Camp, which she says was even more memorable than Everest. She writes that her original *crazy decision to go to Everest ... has contributed to a huge shift in everything I do.*

What are your dreams? Is there something you've secretly longed to do? Might you draw inspiration from Sheila's story and start making plans to make it real?

*To regret fully is to appreciate how high the stakes are
in even the average human life;
fully experienced,
it turns our eyes attentive and alert,
to a future possibly lived better than our past.*
David Whyte

*Nothing has a stronger influence psychologically on their
environment and especially on their children than the
unlived life of the parent.*
C.G. Jung

Tip 22: Don't Ask "WHY?"

Some people see things as they are and say 'why'?
I dream things that never were and say 'why not'?
George Bernard Shaw

Why did that happen to me?
Why did he say that to me?
Why can't I do things better?
Why do I always fail?
Why me?

Asking 'why?' is our way of trying to make sense of things. In its way it can be useful, but 'why' questions can also mire us down, keep us stuck in the past and prevent us from taking action and moving forward.

If you're not careful they can spiral downwards into negative, self-recriminatory thinking which doesn't benefit anyone.

You'll find it's generally much more helpful to ask 'what' questions instead. 'What' questions are assertive and proactive. They're solution-focused; they release energy and move you from feeling stuck into the realm of what's possible. For example ...

Why aren't I better at this? (becomes)
  What can I do to improve?

Why is this happening to me? (becomes)
   What do I want to do about it?

Why didn't I handle that better? (becomes)
   What can I learn from this?

Why me? (becomes)
   What do I need to take responsibility for?

Can you see how much more powerful 'what' questions can be? Here are some useful ones:

- ➤ What's the ideal outcome?
- ➤ What do I really want?
- ➤ What's the first step?
- ➤ What are the options?
- ➤ What's stopping me?
- ➤ What's the worst that could happen?

For the next few days, notice what happens when you use the word 'why' and how it makes you feel. Then try asking a different question, this time starting with the word 'what...' My guess is that you'll notice quite a difference.

*Using "what" questions provides the opportunity to start
you along the road to accessing your own wisdom.*
Laura Berman Fortgang

*We will discover the nature of our particular genius
when we stop trying to conform to our own or to
other peoples' models, learn to be ourselves, and allow
our natural channel to open.*
Shakti Gawain

65

Tip 23: Six Steps at a Time

A journey of a thousand miles begins with a single step.
Lao Tzu

Have you ever faced a project or challenge that feels utterly overwhelming? Something that looms so large that it's actually easier NOT to undertake it at all — or at least to keep putting it off?

A few weeks ago I went for a long walk with some friends. At about the half way mark we emerged from some woods and our final destination came into view. The point we were aiming for was a stand of trees at the top of one of the highest spots on the Wiltshire Downs. Not only did it look *miles* away, but our return journey was almost all uphill.

As we trudged on, feeling somewhat daunted and muttering about the distance we still had to go, one of our party recounted this story:

Once upon a time there was a traveller who was on a long, long journey. After many days he reached the top of a mountain and from there he was able to see his destination in the far distance.

He sighed in despair because it seemed so very far away and there were many dangerous rivers and hills to navigate on the way. He felt so overwhelmed by the task in hand that he sank down onto a large rock and held his head in his hands. He sat there for a very long time — until the sun had gone down and the moon had risen in the night sky.

When he looked up again he was startled to see an old man standing before him.
"Why are you so dejected?" the man asked.

The traveller explained his situation and the old man nodded his head in a way that indicated that he understood.

"Here, take this," he said and handed the traveller a torch.
"What is this for?" the traveller asked, standing and holding the torch out in front of him.

"That is a magic torch" said the old man. "It will illuminate your way, but it will only ever shine six steps in front of you. The answer to your predicament is not to think about the distance you have to travel — or where you are headed — but to concentrate merely on the six steps in front of you. Take your journey six steps at a time. The torch will light your way and you will get to your final destination."

Whatever you may be facing in your life that feels daunting and unmanageable, just remember the magic torch and take it six steps at a time.

True life is lived when tiny changes occur.
Leo Tolstoy

Whoever wants to reach a distant goal
must take small steps.
Helmut Schmidt

Tip 24: Trying it On

It doesn't matter which side of the fence you get off on sometimes. What matters most is getting off.
You cannot make progress without making decisions.
Jim Rohn

Some decisions are cut and dried. There's little doubt that one particular course of action is the right one and that makes the decision easy. If only all decisions were like that. More often than not there isn't an obvious answer — several solutions seem plausible and it's easy to become paralysed by the fear of making the *wrong* decision.

If you're faced with a tough decision and no one way is clear, a strategy I often recommend is to *try on* each of the options. Make the decision in your mind, and then *act as if* you're going to go through with it and see how it feels. This way you don't have to burn any bridges, but you get the opportunity of living with the decision for a while to see what it feels like.

Not too long ago I had to make the difficult decision to have our much-loved cat put to sleep. I'd wrestled with it for a long time, but eventually more and more evidence was stacking up and I was feeling under increasing pressure to act. On Monday I called the vet's office to make the appointment for Wednesday. I was *trying it on* to see how it felt and with each passing hour I became more certain that the decision was the right one. I could have changed my mind at any time and walked away from that choice if it really hadn't felt right.

Now, even though we miss him terribly I know I did, in the end, make the right decision and I do believe that it helped to 'live it' for a couple of days first.

Once you make a decision,
the universe conspires to make it happen.
Ralph Waldo Emerson

The greatest mistake you can make in life is to be
continually fearing you will make one.
Elbert Hubbard

Tip 25: How to Stop Wasting Time and Get More Done

One cannot manage too many affairs: like pumpkins in the water, one pops up while you try to hold down the other.
Chinese Proverb

As a Life Coach, one of the complaints I hear most often is 'there aren't enough hours in the day to do all the things I've got to do.' If that sounds familiar, here are some tips to help you use your time as productively as possible.

Get it out of your head and onto paper
It's impossible to be focused when you're overwhelmed by all the things you've got to do. It's even worse when everything is swimming around in your head. One way to combat this is to sit down at the beginning of each working day (or the night before) and make a list of everything you need to do. If there are jobs that are urgent and have to be done today, highlight them and make sure they're done first. If you don't take control of your to-do list you'll spend your time being reactive rather than proactive and that isn't a productive use of your time.

Set your priorities — daily
Once you've written your list try to categorise your tasks into no more than three key priorities. Ask yourself, *what are the three most important things I want today to be about?* For example, one priority might be making phone

calls, another writing reports, while a third could be preparing for an important meeting. Being clear about your priorities helps to focus the mind and stops you from getting distracted. Of course there are bound to be interruptions: when these pop up, check in with yourself to see whether a) they have to be dealt with urgently and b) they will be supportive of one of your three key priorities. If yes, deal with them, if not, postpone them.

Keep a lid on time wasters

We all have activities which, if we're not careful, can consume vast chunks of our valuable time. For many, the chief culprit is *checking email*. Avoid this by giving yourself a strict time limit for Time Wasting Tasks like email and phone calls. We work much more effectively when we know we have a deadline, so setting a timer for, say 20 minutes (and knowing you only have 20 minutes to work on the task) will mean that you attack it with considerably more focus and concentration. I guarantee that doing this one thing will stop you wasting time and significantly increase your productivity.

And finally ...

While it may seem counter-intuitive, don't forget to schedule time for breaks as well. Taking regular, short breaks is guaranteed to refresh you and enhance your effectiveness.

It's easy to be busy. It takes a lot more time, thought and planning to make sure you're using your time effectively and productively.

Everyone has time if he likes.
Business runs after nobody:
People cling to it of their own free will and think that
to be busy is a proof of happiness.
Seneca

Productivity is never an accident.
It is always the result of a commitment to excellence,
intelligent planning, and focused effort.
Paul J Meyer

Even if you are on the right track,
you'll get run over if you just sit there.
Will Rogers

Tip 26: Boost Your Confidence

*Once you replace negative thoughts with positive ones,
you'll start having positive results.*
Willie Nelson

Everyone has their ups and downs. No matter how confident
we may seem on the outside, I don't know anyone who's
100% confident all the time. While many of us sail along
most of the time feeling pretty much OK, every now and
again things can conspire to shake our confidence and our
sense of self.

The word confidence comes from the Latin *confidere*, which
means to *have full trust*. Confidence is about having faith in
yourself — in your qualities and your abilities — and trusting
that whatever life throws at you, you'll be able to handle it.
So when our confidence falters, how do we recalibrate?
What can we do to restore our equilibrium? Here are some
ideas:

➤ First and foremost be really good to yourself. This may
sound trite, but when our confidence is shaky we can be
unreasonably hard on ourselves and give ourselves a tough
time for 'not doing better'. So a good way to start building
your confidence is to practice some *extreme self-care*. Put
yourself at the top of the list, nurture and be kind to
yourself.

➤ The New Oxford Dictionary defines confidence as: *A feeling of self-assurance arising from one's appreciation of one's own abilities or qualities.* With this in mind, write a list of 10 things you like about yourself and think you do well.

➤ Create a 'Feel Good' Box and fill it with positive, encouraging notes, emails, letters, certificates, pictures — anything that makes you feel good and reminds you how brilliant you are. Reach for this box whenever you feel your confidence is waning.

➤ Spend as little time as possible with those who criticise you or undermine your confidence. The messages we receive from those around us can affect how we feel about ourselves, so choosing not to be around those who erode our confidence is really important. Surround yourself with people who love and support you and encourage you to succeed.

➤ Give yourself a quick confidence boost by getting a new hair-cut, throwing out a piece of clothing that's old and baggy and doesn't suit you and buying something new — or upgrading your immediate environment in some way. These external factors can affect how we feel internally.

➤ Watch your language. If you're feeling a bit low you might be tempted to put yourself down in front of other people — resist at all costs! If this is the message you're giving out to the world, it will be having a negative impact on you, too.

➤ Confidence comes from taking action and the very best way to boost your confidence is to challenge yourself and step out of your comfort zone. So set yourself a couple of 'stretch' goals: it may feel uncomfortable, but your confidence will soar when you achieve them.

When the grass looks greener on the other side of the
fence, it may be that they take better care of it there.
Cecil Selig

When there is no enemy within,
the enemies outside cannot hurt you.
African Proverb

Shyness has a strange element of narcissism,
a belief that how we look, how we perform,
is truly important to other people.
André Dubus

Tip 27: Getting Feedback

He who knows others is wise;
he who knows himself is enlightened.
Lao Tzu

The way we see ourselves is often at odds with the way others see us. Equally, sometimes it can be hard for us to appreciate our innate abilities simply because they come so naturally to us. Being a superb organiser or a natural teacher or a whizz at numbers is so effortless for us, we don't recognise it as one of our strengths.

Finding out how others perceive us can be a real eye-opener and a great way to tap into our strengths and natural abilities. This is particularly useful if you're contemplating a career change. One of the ways to do this is to ask for feedback. This may feel a bit daunting, but it's a very affirming exercise and you may be amazed at how perceptive and wise those around you can be. Select at least five people who know you — ideally from different areas of your life (family, work colleague, friend, social contact, etc.) Be sure to choose people you can trust to give you honest, constructive feedback and ask them to answer some or all of the following questions:

➢ *What do you like/value most about me?*

➢ *What aspect of my personality would you most like to change and why?*

➤ *What do you perceive to be my greatest strengths / natural gifts?*

➤ *What do you think my greatest accomplishments are?*

➤ *How do you think I come across to new people?*

➤ *What could I do, if anything, to give people a better impression of me?*

Feel free to add other questions. For example, if you're thinking of changing career, you could ask 'What kind of job/work do you think would suit me?'

You don't have to ask the questions directly — sending them by email allows people to respond in their own time.

When you've received the feedback, collate the information and look for common themes.

➤ How many of the opinions you received reinforce each other?

➤ Is there anything that particularly surprises you in the answers you received?

➤ Is there a difference between how other people see you and how you see yourself?

➤ What insights have you gained from this exercise?

➤ How will you change your life so as to build on your natural strengths?

➤ Can you start to connect with your source of power?

Remember — *awareness is the precursor of change.* Once you're aware of a particular trait or behaviour you can choose to embrace it, or change it if you want to.

We don't know who we are until
we can see what we can do.
Martha Grimes

An honest answer is a sign of true friendship.
Proverbs

The only service a friend can really render is to keep up
your courage by holding up to you a mirror in which you can
see a noble image of yourself.
George Bernard Shaw

Tip 28: Pictures at an Exhibition

Art does not reproduce what we see;
rather, it makes us see.
Paul Klee

Every year in July and August the Royal Academy in London holds its Summer Exhibition. It's a unique exhibition, as it gives unknown artists the opportunity to be exhibited alongside the heavyweights of the art world. It's also wonderfully diverse: painting, sculpture, drawings, prints, photography, architectural models, installations and prices ranging from hundreds to hundreds of thousands of pounds.

Wandering the galleries last year, it struck me that visiting an exhibition (especially one as varied as the RA) is an excellent way to learn, naturally and instinctively, more about yourself. What do I mean?

I noticed that I was instinctively drawn to certain types of subject matter. Regardless of the media, it was the artworks that depicted people — particularly those with some sort of obscure back-story — that attracted me most. This shouldn't come as too much of a surprise: my work as a coach is based on a love of people and is all about finding out more about their stories and helping them to realise the best of themselves.

But I was intrigued to notice that I was also drawn to pictures of trees. I adore trees and, if I had my life to live again, perhaps I'd have chosen to work with wood in some way. This was the light-bulb moment when I realised how personally revealing an exhibition can be and how it could throw light on future career choices.

One of the things I help clients with is to figure out what kind of work they will find satisfying and enjoyable. There are lots of 'thinking' exercises they can work through to come up with ideas of what they'll enjoy, what they're naturally good at and what will make them happy.

But it struck me that wandering around an exhibition and simply noticing what you're attracted to might be an instinctive, and much more fun, way to uncover some ideas.

I tried out my theory on my brother and sister as we sat with a coffee after visiting the exhibition. My brother was attracted to landscapes, which absolutely complements his love of the countryside and long distance walking. My sister said that she had been drawn to the abstract pieces, which was a surprise to her as this wasn't normally the case. At first she struggled to make a connection and then realised that in fact she is entering a more cerebral phase of her life and thinking about things in a more abstract way.

Fascinating.

So as we roll into summer, and if you're searching for clues about what makes you tick, why not take in an exhibition or two. Notice what you're drawn to. After all, what we find interesting in art may be an indication, at the most basic and fundamental level, of who we are.

Art is the essence of awareness.
Louise Nevelson

One looks, looks long, and the world comes in.
Joseph Campbell

I have the feeling that I've seen everything,
but failed to notice the elephants.
Anton Chekhov

Tip 29: Never Ever Give Up

In the confrontation between the stream and the rock,
the stream always wins — not through strength
but by perseverance.
H. Jackson Brown

Lang Lang is one of the most successful pianists of his generation. He performed before a global audience of four and a half billion at the opening ceremony of the Beijing Olympics. He sells out concerts wherever he plays and is beloved by audiences world-wide. He was a child prodigy and extraordinary talent — yet he almost gave up playing the piano when he was nine years old.

I was shocked to hear him recount the story of how he was told by his piano teacher that he had no talent — that he would never make it and should give up playing the piano. So distraught was he by this rejection (and his father's harsh response to his 'failure') that he tried to destroy his hands by hitting them against a wall. It's truly shocking to think that this phenomenal talent could have been extinguished and stamped out before it had the opportunity to flourish and be appreciated in the world.

If there was ever an example of how vital it is to persist in the face of criticism and rejection then surely this is it. There are many others: The original Harry Potter manuscript by J.K. Rowling was rejected umpteen times before it was finally published; it took years of persistence before James

Dyson's innovative bag-less vacuum cleaner was finally manufactured and made millions.

It's all too easy to be dissuaded or knocked off course by the views of others — especially if you're not feeling too confident yourself. But don't be deflected.

Is there something you feel passionate about doing but you've given up because of negative comments or rejection by others? If you're not sure, revisit the 80th Birthday visualisation in Tip 21 and see if anything comes up. Or try completing the sentence *'If I really had my way I'd ...'*

Go for it. Persist. Life's too short not to follow your passion.

Obstacles don't have to stop you.
If you run into a wall, don't turn around and give up.
Figure out how to climb it, go through it,
or work around it.
Michael Jordan

Not hammer-strokes, but dance of the water,
sings the pebbles into perfection.
Rabindranath Tagore

Our greatest weakness lies in giving up.
The most certain way to succeed is
always to try just one more time.
Thomas Alva Edison

Tip 30: Outrageous Goal Setting

You have powers you never dreamed of.
You can do things you never thought you could do.
There are no limitations in what you can do except
the limitations of your own mind.
Darwin P. Kingsley

Sometimes it can be just too boring — too safe — to go with the standard SMART formula for goals. According to the SMART formula, when setting yourself a goal you should make sure it is

S = Specific
M = Measurable
A = Achievable
R = Realistic
T = Time Defined

I agree that a goal needs to be specific, measurable and time defined. For example, setting a goal *to lose weight* isn't nearly as effective as saying *I'm going to lose 10 pounds by my friend's wedding in June*. It gives you something specific to aim for by a certain date and you can measure your progress. So far so good. It is true, too, that goals need to be achievable and realistic. But sometimes setting yourself a totally outrageous and crazy goal can be far more motivating.

This book is a good example. Last year, on a bit of a whim, I went for a reading with an astrologer friend of mine. She told me that this was a great time to get new projects up and running, and that writing and communication were really well favoured. When I mentioned that I'd been thinking of writing a new book, her eyes lit up and she said that this would be the perfect time. Scrutinising further aspects of my chart she informed me with a smile that I had seven days to do it!

Galvanised by this absolutely ludicrous target, I went home and worked solidly. My focus was absolute and ten days later the book you're reading now was about 60% finished. I have absolutely no doubt that what galvanised me into action was having such an outrageous goal to achieve.

QUESTION: Would it inspire you to set yourself a completely outrageous goal? If so, what? And if not now, when?

Don't be afraid to take a big step if one is indicated.
You can't cross a chasm in two small jumps.
David Lloyd George

Ordinary people believe only in the possible.
Extraordinary people visualize not what is possible or
probable, but rather what is impossible.
And by visualizing the impossible,
they begin to see it as possible.
Cherie Carter-Scott

Shoot for the moon.
Even if you miss it you will land among the stars.
Les Brown

Tip 31: Have you joined the Karma Army?

Kindness can become its own motive.
We are made kind by being kind.
Eric Hoffer

In 2002 humourist Danny Wallace placed an ad in a London magazine. The ad said, quite simply, '*JOIN ME*'. To his amazement, hundreds of people responded, even though the ad gave no details at all about what they would be joining, or why. This, in itself, says shed-loads about our need for community and our need to belong to something... but I digress.

Having got such a great response, Wallace then needed to decide what exactly his respondents were joining. His solution was to encourage all his Joinees (his Karma Army as he called them) to undertake Random Acts of Kindness at least once a week. The only instructions were that you had to be nice to someone else for absolutely no personal gain.

Doing nice things for other people has even more impact when it's completely unexpected: paying for the cup of tea that the person in the queue in front of you has just ordered ... offering to carry someone's shopping for them ... sending a friend a card to let them know you're thinking of them ... or even simply holding a door open for someone.

Since then many thousands of people from all over the world have joined the cause. Wallace says *"If what goes around really does come around, we all stand to benefit from these Random Acts of Kindness."*

Small acts of kindness for no personal gain — what a great idea. It's good to feel that a single considerate act has the potential to multiply many times over, and there's no knowing where that could lead.

As the Tibetan Buddhist monk Patrul Rinpoche put it so well:

> *Do not take lightly small good deeds,*
> *believing they can hardly help.*
> *For drops of water, one by one,*
> *in time can fill a giant pot.*

Human kindness has never weakened the stamina
or softened the fiber of a free people.
A nation does not have to be cruel to be tough.
Franklin D. Roosevelt

One who knows how to show and to accept kindness will be
a friend better than any possession.
Sophocles

Give nobody's heart pain so long as thou canst avoid it,
for one sigh may set a whole world into a flame.
Sa'di

Tip 32: 'Doing a Scarlett'

The distance is nothing;
it's only the first step that is difficult.
Marquise du Deffand

Do you develop an Ostrich Mentality when you have an issue weighing on your mind or a difficult decision to make? You know you ought to face it head on, but it's so much easier to bury your head in the sand and make yourself super-busy as a way to avoid having to think about it.

I call this *Doing a Scarlett,* because Scarlett O'Hara exhibited exactly the same mind-set in the final scene of the movie Gone with the Wind. When Rhett Butler finally leaves her, she cries in her fabulous Southern drawl: *I can't let him go. I can't. There must be some way to bring him back. Oh, I can't think about that right now! I'll go crazy if I do! I'll think about it tomorrow.*

It's often so much easier to think about it tomorrow than face it today. But you can't get away from the fact that the issue is still there. Every now and again it will creep into your mind, your heart will sink, your energy will drain just a little but it still feels easier to avoid it by finding some easy, routine task that absolutely **has** to be done — immediately! That way you can put off the issue just a bit longer. Until the next time it resurfaces.

As with all forms of procrastination, we're not avoiding the issue itself — we're avoiding taking the first step towards dealing with it. So if you find yourself *Doing a Scarlett* and avoiding an issue in your life, try this exercise:

Sit down with a pen and some paper. Write your issue, challenge or a decision you need to make as a heading at the top of the page. Set a timer for five minutes and just start writing. It doesn't matter if what you write doesn't make sense — it doesn't matter if it's full of spelling mistakes. Nobody else has to read it. The key is to get your thoughts out of your head and down on paper.

When the timer goes off after five minutes stop writing and look back over what you've written. Underline or highlight anything you feel is important or relevant.

The crucial thing is that you've started the ball rolling. The issue is no longer an amorphous, undefined fog in your head — it's started to take shape and you've taken the first step to face it and deal with it. Hopefully this will give you the impetus you need to get to grips with the problem.

QUESTION: What are YOU avoiding - right now?

It is not because things are difficult that we do not dare;
it is because we do not dare that they are difficult.
Seneca

The greatest amount of wasted time
is the time not getting started.
Dawson Trotman

Tip 33: The 80 / 20 Rule

What is the use of running when we are
not on the right road?
German Proverb

In his book, The 4-Hour Work Week, Timothy Ferriss describes how he managed to radically boost his income while working for a fraction of the time. One of the ways he did this was to use the 80/20 Rule (the Pareto Principle) which states that 80% of results typically come from 20% of our effort and time. Ferriss scrutinised his business, asking himself the following questions:

➢ Which 20% of sources are causing 80% of my problems and unhappiness?
➢ Which 20% of sources are resulting in 80% of my desired outcomes and happiness?

From this analysis he figured out that almost all his income was generated from just a small proportion of his clients. Not only that, but there were a handful of clients who consistently caused problems and wasted his time and energy. He dropped the clients who were causing him problems, stopped focusing on the majority of clients who rarely placed orders and spent almost all his time and effort developing the clients who generated the most income. As a result his income doubled in the first month and his weekly hours dropped from 80 to 15. Not a bad outcome!

Take a long hard look at the things on your daily to-do list. Are you focusing on the 20% of activities that will reap rewards and bring you increased income and happiness? Or are you concentrating on time wasters? Are you using your time effectively or are you just 'being busy'?

Maybe it's time to focus your attention on the 20% and to apply the 'Three Ds Rule' (Do it, Delegate it, Drop it) for the rest. In other words, Do the 20% and consider what part of the 80% you can Delegate or Drop altogether.

The 80/20 Rule can be a life saver for perfectionists, too. When you're striving for that perfect 100%, check in with yourself and see if, actually, 80% would do. This single shift can save you loads of time and energy.

Minimalism is essentially focusing only on the 3-4 most important things in your life (or business) and ELIMINATING THE REST.
John Reese

The ability to simplify means to eliminate the unnecessary so that the necessary may speak.
Hans Hofmann

The secret of happiness, you see, is not found in seeking more, but in developing the capacity to enjoy less.
Socrates

Tip 34: The Miracle Question

Identify your problems,
but give your power and energy to solutions.
Anthony Robbins

As its name suggests, Solutions Focus Coaching concentrates not on problems, but looks instead at what's already working for solutions. The theory is based on these three common-sense principles:

1. If it ain't broke, don't fix it
2. Once you know what works, do more of it, and
3. Stop doing what doesn't work and do something different.

At the heart of Solutions Focus coaching is the Miracle Question, which is asked early on in the process to elicit the Ideal Outcome and to draw out any existing solutions to the current problem or issue. Here's a simplified version of the Solutions Focus process that you can try for yourself.

▶ Think of a problem or challenge you're facing right now.

▶ Ask yourself the Miracle Question:

Suppose that tonight you go to bed and go to sleep as usual. But during the night a miracle happens. Your problem vanishes and the issues that have been worrying you are resolved. But because you're asleep you don't know that the miracle has happened. So... when you wake up tomorrow what will be the first indications that tell you the miracle has taken place? What will be different? What changes will you notice? How will you know that the transformation has occurred? What will you be doing? What will you be saying? What will other people notice? What else?

▶ On a scale of 0-10 where 10 is the Ideal as described above and 0 is the worst things have ever been — where are you now? (Let's say you're at a 4). What's helped you to get to a 4? What are you already doing to achieve that score? When have you experienced even a part of the ideal? What was happening then? (Here you're looking for resources and skills you already possess and can use more of to help overcome your current issue).

▶ Ask yourself what small step could you take in the next couple of days to get you a little further up the scale — say to a 4.5 or a 5? What would be the first small signs of progress?

▶ Finally, keep reviewing your progress by asking *What's better?*

Sometimes we can be so bogged down in our problems that seeing a way out feels impossible. The Miracle Question is a really handy way to take yourself out of the problem and, by focusing on your ideal outcome, start the journey towards a resolution.

Don't dwell on what went wrong.
Instead, focus on what to do next.
Spend your energies on moving forward toward
finding the answer.
Denis Waitley

Worry is like a rocking chair — it gives you something to do
but won't get you anywhere.
Unknown Author

The significant problems we face cannot be solved at the
same level of thinking we were at when we created them.
Albert Einstein

Tip 35: Kicking the Habit

I have discovered that we may be in some degree
whatever character we choose.
Besides, practice forms a man to anything.
James Boswell

Bad habits are tough to break. After all, they've probably become ingrained over many years. But I believe that we can change any behaviour we want to, given a solid intention and a liberal dose of willpower.

I've been putting this belief to the test recently. One of my worst habits is my tendency to snack. Give me a packet of crisps before supper or a bar of chocolate after lunch and I have the willpower of a damp cardboard box. As I wanted to lose a few pounds I decided drastic action needed to be taken. To help keep me on the straight and narrow, and to practice putting some new habits in place, I used a simple coaching exercise called Ten Daily Habits.

This is how it works:

1. Draw a grid — 8 columns wide and up to 11 deep.

2. In the left-hand column list up to 10 things that you want to do (or not do) on a daily basis. (I specified seven things, including *no chocolate after lunch; no food after 8pm; walk round the block at lunchtime; practice T'ai Ch'i* and *drink lemon water first thing in the morning*.)

3. Along the top, write the days of the week — Monday to Sunday.

4. Each day, as you achieve the goal you've set yourself you can have the pleasure and satisfaction of ticking the box. This reinforces the positive behaviour and should help to keep you motivated.

Here's my example:

	Monday	Tuesday	Wednesday	Thursday	Friday	Saturday	Sunday
No Chocolate	√	√		√		√	
Lemon Water		√	√		√		
No food after 8pm	√		√	√		√	√
Walk	√	√	√	√	√	√	
Play piano	√		√		√	√	
Tai Chi		√	√	√		√	
Write Journal	√	√		√		√	√

This exercise really works for me. The crazy thing is that even though it's only a piece of paper — and a piece of paper that only I will see — I honestly feel that I have to succeed so that I can Tick the Box.

You don't have to stick to daily habits — some people find it useful to do weekly habits instead, or even a combination of the two.

After you've done a thing the same way for two years,
look it over carefully.
After five years, look at it with suspicion.
And after ten years, throw it away and start all over.
Alfred Edward Perlman

Yesterday is not ours to recover,
but tomorrow is ours to win or lose.
Lyndon B. Johnson

Tip 36: Do Yourself Differently

If you want to be different,
Perhaps the answer is to become different yourself.
Normal Vincent Peale

A few years ago I attended a wonderful personal development workshop called The Mastery. One of the themes that ran through the workshop was the intriguing invitation to *Do Yourself Differently*. It was an opportunity to experiment by being different from your normal self.

For example, when the time came for introductions, those who would normally get up first so as to get it over and done with, were invited to try waiting until last to see what that felt like — and vice versa. Those who naturally tended towards taking care of others' needs before their own were invited to spend the weekend asking others for what they needed. Those who tended to be quiet and blend into the background were invited to be really 'out there' and to make their presence well and truly felt.

This invitation had profound consequences. It's such a simple idea, but holds within it so many possibilities for creativity, expansion and enrichment. The more I thought about this the more I decided that the concept of doing myself differently was something I wanted to carry forward into my life. It set me thinking about the way I spend my time, the way my business is structured and my work-life balance and how I could do that differently.

How would *you* like to do yourself differently?

If you've come back from the summer break feeling refreshed, invigorated and ready for something new, then maybe you, too, feel ready and willing to embrace this concept. Conversely, if you're feeling a bit sluggish and down-hearted at the thought of getting back to your normal routine after a holiday, then what better way to shake things up a bit and step out of the same old, same old...

In her book *Feel The Fear and Do It Anyway*, Susan Jeffers suggests planning and taking daily risks as a way to move away from fear and step into your personal power. A risk doesn't have to be major — it could simply be trying something you've not done before, or don't feel entirely comfortable with. Jeffers says that taking risks (no matter how small) and edging out of your comfort zone builds your confidence and sense of strength and power.

In the same way, 'doing yourself differently' is an invitation to experiment: to try out new things; to do and be something different; to play a bit and get creative. It may feel awkward and uncomfortable, but it's guaranteed to be invigorating.

*What lies behind us and what lies before
us are tiny matters, compared to what lies within us.*
Ralph Waldo Emerson

*We cannot escape fear.
We can only transform it into a companion
that accompanies us on all our exciting adventures ...
Take a risk a day – one small or bold stroke
that will make you feel great once you have done it.*
Susan Jeffers

Tip 37: Pause ...

Never be in a hurry; do everything quietly
and in a calm spirit.
Do not lose your inner peace for anything whatsoever,
even if your whole world seems upset.
Saint Francis de Sales

Pause ...

For 10 seconds to take a deep breath
For 1 minute to take in the view
For a couple of minutes to brew a cuppa
For 10 minutes to clear your head
For 20 minutes to call your Mum
For half an hour to exercise your body
For a couple of hours to read a good book
For a day to find some fun
For a weekend under the stars
For a fortnight to recharge your batteries
For a month to learn something new
For a summer to be a kid again
For a year to see the world
For a lifetime to work out what it all means
Or for five minutes to do absolutely nothing.

Alastair Humphreys

To get all there is out of living,
we must employ our time wisely,
never being in too much of a hurry to stop and sip life,
but never losing our sense of the
enormous value of a minute.
Robert Updegraff

I were better to be eaten to death with a rust than to be
scoured to nothing with perpetual motion.
Shakespeare

Tip 38: Develop an Optimism Habit

The average pencil is seven inches long, with
just a half-inch eraser –
in case you thought optimism was dead.
Robert Brault

There are lots of good reasons to practice an optimistic outlook. Not only do optimists tend to achieve more and are less likely to suffer from stress and depression — they've been shown to live longer and recover more quickly from illness.

Are you a glass half full or a glass half empty person? If you tend towards pessimism, there is hope. Optimism is something that can be learned. Here are a few ways to help change your thinking style and develop an optimism habit:

▶ At the end of each day, write a list, or make a mental note, of everything you've achieved that day. Don't limit it only to 'big' things: *remembering to post Dad's birthday card* deserves to be on the list as much as *finally got my promotion at work*. Focusing on achievements is a great habit to get into. It's a way of appreciating yourself and curbs any natural inclination to get to the end of the day wondering what on earth you've achieved, or focusing (as pessimists are wont to do) on everything you've failed to do — or haven't done as well as you'd have liked. Keep this up for at least two weeks and you should notice a real difference.

► Thinking about what's been good about the day last thing at night has other benefits too. It releases the chemical serotonin in the brain, which helps us to relax and sleep better.

► Take a tip from the Solutions Focus camp (see Tip 34 The Miracle Question) and keep asking yourself What's Better? Maybe you could schedule a time at the end of each week to do this.

Focusing on the positive not only helps to encourage optimism, it lessens stress and is likely to make us a lot nicer to be around.

A pessimist sees the difficulty in every opportunity;
an optimist sees the opportunity in every difficulty.
Winston Churchill

A positive attitude may not solve all your problems,
but it will annoy enough people to
make it worth the effort.
Herm Albright

Most of the shadows of this life are
caused by standing in one's own sunshine.
Ralph Waldo Emerson

Tip 39: Unfinished Business

In hell there is no other punishment
than to begin over and over again
the tasks left unfinished in your lifetime.
André Gide

In matters artistic, there's something mysterious and romantic about things that are unfinished. There's a certain allure and fascination about an unfinished symphony, novel or painting.

However, in everyday life there's nothing at all alluring about things that are unfinished — quite the opposite, in fact. They sap your energy and leave you feeling frustrated, bad tempered and drained.

Are there things in your life that are 'unfinished'?
➤ Half-finished work projects?
➤ A room in the house that's only half decorated?
➤ An incomplete short story or novel?
➤ A course of learning embarked on but abandoned?
➤ A letter half written?
➤ A book half read?
➤ Do you have any unfinished business with a former partner, friend or colleague?

Make a list of all those unfinished items and decide once and for all whether you want to complete them, delegate them or drop them. Some projects can be left for so long that we no longer have the enthusiasm for them that we once did. They may have become irrelevant or no longer aligned with who we are or what we want in life.

I challenge you this week to take steps to eliminate all the unfinished stuff in your life. I guarantee it will make a big difference to the way you feel.

Two things rob people of their peace of mind;
work unfinished and work not yet begun.
Alexander Solzhenitsyn

There is nothing so fatal to character as half-finished tasks.
David Lloyd George

It's not so important who starts the game
but who finishes it.
John Wooden

Tip 40: Three Simple Goals

October is the fallen leaf, but it is also
a wider horizon more clearly seen.
It is the distant hills once more in sight,
and the enduring constellations above them once again.
Hal Borland

Somehow, almost without my noticing it, we've edged into October. For many of us the summer holidays are already a distant memory, we're back at work and life is rushing by at its usual relentless pace, allowing little time for reflection. The days are getting shorter and before we know it Christmas will be here and with it the end of the year.

This makes it an ideal time to do some planning for the last quarter of the year.

Some years ago I took part in a coaching Mastermind Group and I remember the facilitator of the group asking us this question at around this time of year: *Looking forward to December, what do you need to do in the next three months to feel that you've reached the end of the year with a real sense of accomplishment?*

It's a clever question in that it makes you think yourself forward to the end of the year and to consider how it would feel — and what would be different — if you had that sense of accomplishment.

Here's another way to approach the same question:

Step One
Write down three goals that you feel would significantly improve your life — personally and/or professionally — in the next 90 days. Check in with yourself to make sure these are goals that genuinely invigorate and motivate you — not goals you feel you *should* do.

Step Two
Once you've decided on your goals, divide each one up into smaller action steps and give each one a start and a finish date. Don't forget to leave space for a tick box so that you can tick each step as you complete it — always motivating.

By doing this simple exercise you should end up with a focus and an action plan for the next three months, taking you into December with a satisfying feeling of accomplishment.

To understand the heart and mind of a person,
look not at what he has already achieved,
but at what he aspires to.
Kahlil Gibran

Many people fail in life,
not for lack of ability or brains or even courage
but simply because they have never organized
their energies around a goal.
Elbert Hubbard

Tip 41: What's Your Mantra?

"I am the greatest!"
Muhammad Ali

Some years ago I heard a radio report from an orphanage in Africa which was devoted to caring for children who had lost both parents to HIV/AIDS. The director of the orphanage was explaining that one of their primary aims was to build up the children's confidence and self-belief in order to enable them to make their way successfully in the wider world.

The children had written their own theme song which they sang every morning. The words of the chorus were, quite simply *"I am special – I am beautiful – I am clever"* and they sang the words with such gusto, such joy, such energy that you felt they truly believed every syllable.

Their song was a simple but powerful reminder that what we believe about ourselves – both positive and negative – can have a major impact on our lives, on how others perceive us, and how we perceive ourselves.

So here's an experiment: like the children, choose your own empowering mantra (something you really need to hear) and practice using it this week. Speak it out loud – sing it to yourself – think or chant it before you go to sleep – write it on post-it notes and stick them all over the house. Inhale deeply as you think of your positive statement (literally breathe the good stuff in).

I remember the first time I tried this. My mantra was *I am beautiful*. I repeated the phrase to myself with as much feeling and self-belief as I could muster and it very quickly started to make a discernible difference. I noticed myself standing up straighter, holding my head up high and strangers were even (to my amazement) starting to turn to look at me! I did, truly, start to feel beautiful.

Negative beliefs can be deeply entrenched and it takes time and practice to unstick and replace them with positive ones. Using a series of empowering mantras is a good way to start.

How much longer will you go on letting your energy sleep?
How much longer are you going to stay oblivious
of the immensity of yourself?
Bhagwan Shree Rajneesh

An affirmation is a strong, positive statement that
something is already so.
Shakti Gawain

Oh man! There is no planet, sun or star could hold you,
if you but knew what you are.
Ralph Waldo Emerson

Tip 42: The Obstacle is the Path

If you find a path with no obstacles,
it probably doesn't lead anywhere.
Frank A. Clark

In ancient times, a King had a boulder placed on a roadway. Then he hid himself and watched to see if anyone would remove the huge rock. Some of the king's wealthiest merchants and courtiers came by and simply walked around it. Many loudly blamed the king for not keeping the roads clear, but none did anything about moving the stone out of the way.

Then a peasant came along carrying a load of vegetables. When he reached the boulder, he laid down his burden and tried to move the stone to the side of the road. After considerable pushing and straining, he finally succeeded. As the peasant picked up his vegetables, he noticed a purse lying in the road where the boulder had been. The purse contained many gold coins and a note from the king indicating that the gold was for the person who removed the boulder from the roadway.

The peasant learned a valuable lesson: that every obstacle has within it the potential to improve our situation.

Each time we encounter unexpected challenges or drawbacks in our lives we're presented with a choice. We can dwell on the unfairness of it, or we can choose to see it as a gift and an opportunity. Difficult and uncomfortable though it is, maybe this problem is there to help us to make a change.

Here's a real life example from Sheelagh, who was dealt a tough card when she encountered an unexpected illness. She says:

This illness has been a great teacher and your words about 'the obstacle is the path' has been such an inspiration. I have found out who my real friends are; that I can say 'no' to people and that they will still respect me; that I have the right to be ill and have time off, and that I need to take more time off and have more fun and do more spiritual reading. Another spin-off is that I have bought a juicer to improve my immune system. In a few months I will be great!! Horrid and scary though it has been, only good will come from this.

If you find yourself in challenging circumstances, see if you can see beyond them by asking ...

➢ *What's the opportunity here?*
➢ *What's the gift?*
➢ *What's the lesson / What can I learn?*
➢ *Where are the blessings in this situation?*

Look for the opportunities in the difficulties,
not the difficulties in the opportunities.
Victor Fiorelli

While we stop to think, we often miss our opportunity.
Publilius Syrus

Life's up and downs provide windows of opportunity
to determine your values and goals.
Think of using all obstacles as stepping-stones
to build the life you want.
Marsha Sinetar

Tip 43: Follow the Energy

The more willing you are to surrender to the energy within you, the more power can flow through you.
Shakti Gawain

When faced with decisions and life choices, our natural inclination might be to want to think it through. We analyse, we consider all the angles, we write lists of pros and cons, costs and benefits and so on. We might seek advice from friends and family: what would they do in a similar situation?

Of course it's helpful to do this. But when I'm working with clients I'll listen for the energy in their voices — or lack of it — when we're discussing various options. Sometimes it's glaringly obvious that one course of action holds energy and enthusiasm while another feels heavy, dull and lifeless.

If you find yourself at a crossroads and considering options, *notice where the energy is. Listen to it.* You can't fabricate a sense of natural, intuitive energy.

If you have a decision to make, write all the options on pieces of paper and put them into a box. Draw each one out in turn and, as you read it, be hyper-aware of how you're reacting. Notice what's going on in your body. Does your heart sink or does it sing? Do you feel a sense of excitement, a release of energy? Or do you feel lacklustre and anxious? Pay attention to these feelings. They're intuitive hits — they tell you where the energy is and where your passion lies.

You will recognize your own path when you come upon it,
because you will suddenly have all the energy and
imagination you will ever need.
Jerry Gillies

See where your own energy wants to go,
not where you think it should go.
Do something because it feels right,
not because it makes sense.
Follow the spiritual impulse.
Mary Hayes Grieco

Tip 44: Living Purposefully

Great dancers are not great because of their technique;
they are great because of their passion.
Martha Graham

One of the keys to creating a fulfilling life is to make sure that it's aligned with your purpose and your passion. How to do this? A good place to start is by considering these questions:

What do you value most?
Write a list of all the things you value most. These are the things that are most important to you — which have the most meaning for you and that bring joy to your life. A few examples might be relationships, family, creativity, nature, travel, laughter, adventure, solitude, spirituality, community ...

What are you passionate about?
Think back over your life and write down times when you were doing something you felt passionate about. These are likely to be times when you were completely absorbed, felt you could carry on doing what you were doing indefinitely and didn't notice that hours had passed. These don't have to be highly significant incidents: it could be the simplest thing such as reading a good book or walking in the countryside on a balmy summer's evening.

What are your skills?
Write down everything you're good at and (as they usually go

hand in hand) love doing. Are you good at sports - repairing things - music - making people laugh - business - caring for others - working with children? To get a different perspective (and perhaps add some unexpected items to your list) you could ask friends, family or colleagues for some feedback (see Tip 27 Getting Feedback). Sometimes the things we do well come so naturally to us that we aren't even aware of the gifts we have.

What qualities do you admire in others?
Finally, think of people that you really admire. They can be living or dead, known to you personally or not. The key is to consider what characteristics you admire in each person. What do they symbolise for you? This is an interesting one, because even if two people write down the same person (let's say Winston Churchill) the qualities they admire might be completely different. One might admire his extraordinary leadership while for another his skill as an orator might be the key characteristic for them.

Quite simply, if we can find a way of life that is the living expression of the things we value; the things we feel passionate about; the things we're naturally good at and the qualities we admire in others, we're much more likely to feel that ours is a purposeful life.

Ignoring your passion is like dying a slow death...
Passion whispers to you through your feelings,
beckoning you toward your highest good.
Pay attention to what makes you feel energized,
connected, stimulated –
what gives you your juice.
Do what you love, give it back in the form of service,
and you will do more than succeed. You will triumph.
Oprah Winfrey

People are self-motivated.
They do their best work when they come to believe,
through their own processes, that what they are going to
do is worthwhile.
John Harvey-Jones

Tip 45: What Would You Like to Have Happen?

Outstanding people have one thing in common:
an absolute sense of mission.
Zig Ziglar

When I was starting out as a coach, I remember a session I had with my own coach in which I was complaining at great length about someone who had upset me. I was brimming with indignation about this and my coach was helping me to look at options for dealing with the situation.

I was all set to pick up the phone and speak to the person and, because I was upset and hadn't thought things through properly, would almost certainly have ended up making things worse. But my coach asked me a very wise question: *What's your **purpose** for making this call? What, specifically, do you want to achieve?*

Considering things from that perspective helped me to think things through more objectively and make a considered decision as to how to proceed (I chose not to make the call).

I learned a lot from that coaching session. Rather than blundering mindlessly into things — whether it's a potentially tricky personal conversation or an important business meeting — it always pays to think it through beforehand and be mindful of what you want to achieve from it. What's your purpose? What's your intention? What's your ideal outcome?

Perhaps the best question of all for focusing the mind is the one which is asked at the start of all Clean Language sessions. It really pins you to the wall and makes you focus on your desired outcome ...

What Would You Like To Have Happen?

The world has the habit of making room for the man
whose words and actions show that he
knows where he is going.
Napoleon Hill

There are two things to aim at in life:
first, to get what you want;
and after that, to enjoy it.
Only the wisest of mankind achieve the second.
Logan Pearsall Smith

Tip 46: Extreme Self Respect

*There is a connection between self-nurturing
and self-respect.*
Julia Cameron

Extreme Self Care is something I recommend to clients whenever they're feeling a bit low or down in the dumps. Extreme Self Care means putting yourself first, wrapping yourself up in cotton wool, lots of pampering and generally taking really good care of yourself.

Extreme Self Respect is another nurturing habit to practice. The best thing is that you can apply it to so many different situations, such as:

➢ a reminder to give yourself a treat of some kind
➢ to book that holiday you've been putting off
➢ to look after your health
➢ to choose not to gossip about others
➢ to NOT demolish that huge piece of chocolate cake
➢ to raise your standards at work
➢ to stand up for what you believe in
➢ to say no to something that doesn't serve you
➢ to stick to your values
➢ to maintain strong personal boundaries at home or at work
➢ to make time for what's important to you

We all deserve respect and the best place to start is by respecting ourselves.

Respect your efforts, respect yourself.
Self-respect leads to self-discipline.
When you have both firmly under your belt,
that's real power.
Clint Eastwood

They cannot take away our self-respect
if we do not give it to them.
Mahatma Gandhi

If we lose love and self-respect for each other,
this is how we finally die.
Maya Angelou

Tip 47: From Darkness Into Light

Better to light one small candle
than to curse the darkness.
Chinese Proverb

In November each year an Advent Procession service is held in Salisbury Cathedral. The service begins in total darkness and then gradually, to the sound of sublime choral plainsong, hundreds of candles are lit throughout the vast space of the Cathedral. It's a deeply moving and spiritually uplifting experience.

Advent is, of course, all about the coming of the Light. But we're not far now from the Winter Solstice; that day in the depths of winter that heralds the turning of the earth from winter to spring — from darkness into light.

I found myself reflecting on this during the service and all the different meanings of the coming of the light. For some it will have a profound religious / spiritual significance. For others it may bring a sense of hope and optimism that from that point in December the days will gradually lengthen as we move towards spring; when the natural world stirs and green shoots start to appear above the ground.

But what about the less obvious aspects of moving from darkness into light? Could it be removing the cloak that's kept you covered from the world and stepping into the light of who you really are? Making the brave decision to move out of a job or relationship that's kept you in the dark into

135

one that brings joy and light into your life? Is it giving yourself permission to be who you know you really are — not repressed by the expectations of others? Is it by doing something outrageous to ignite a spark in yourself and in your life? What might that look and feel like?

I will love the sun for it warms my bones;
yet I will love the rain for it cleanses my spirit.
I will love the light for it shows me the way;
yet I will love the darkness for it shows me the stars.
Og Mandino

Darkness cannot drive out darkness; only light can do that.
Hate cannot drive out hate; only love can do that.
Dr Martin Luther King Jr.

Tip 48: Reasons to be Cheerful

*I've found that worry and irritation vanish into thin air
the moment I open my mind to the many blessings I possess.*
Dale Carnegie

When I lived in America I always enjoyed the Thanksgiving holiday which takes place at the end of November. One year I remember a commentator giving his personal viewpoint on this very American holiday. He recalled that, as a child, whenever he was upset about a perceived injustice, his mother would always give him the same advice: "Count your blessings, son." He said that this always had a palliative effect and that when he really thought about it, the irritation (whatever it was) always paled into insignificance against the weight of all he had to be thankful for.

Some years ago, when I was going through a difficult time in my own life and finding it hard to focus on anything positive — let alone find much to give thanks for — a friend recommended the following exercise. I found it challenging but immensely helpful and now I recommend it to others:

Week One
Every day write down one thing that you do well / like about yourself and one thing you feel grateful for.

Week Two
Every day write down two things that you do well / like about yourself and two things you feel grateful for.

Week Three

Every day write down three things that you do well / like about yourself and three things you feel grateful for.

A cinch, you might say. Yes, but the catch is that you aren't allowed to repeat yourself at all. Not in the same week, or at any time in the three weeks.

If you enjoy this exercise you might find it beneficial to keep a daily Gratitude Journal where you sit down at the end of each day and write down all the things you feel grateful for.

It's astonishing how shifting our focus onto the positives can lift the spirits and enhance our sense of optimism and well-being.

Ignorant men don't know what good
they hold in their hands
until they've flung it away.
Sophocles

Feeling grateful or appreciative of someone
or something in your life
actually attracts more of the things
that you appreciate and value into your life.
Christiane Northrup

Tip 49: Fertile Void

*In the beginning there was a clay pit with no level ground —
below the water table — with no soil.
A scarred landscape? Or an opportunity to build Eden?*
The Eden Project

Many years ago I received some wise advice from a fellow student on the Masters Degree course in Counselling I was taking in California. At the time I was wrestling with a tough decision. Should I, or should I not walk away from a long-term relationship? I'd been struggling with this decision for so long that I had become completely paralysed. To me there was no clear answer and the more I thought about it, the more I seemed to be going round and round in circles.

I remember explaining to Barbara that what scared me about leaving the relationship was that I'd be left with a giant void. No-one special in my life and that frightened me.

After a few moment's silence Barbara asked if it would make a difference if, instead of thinking of it as a scary, empty void, perhaps I could think of it as a fertile void instead?

A fertile void, where new things can take root and grow. What a brilliant concept.

There are times in life when we have to take risks and let go of those things we know in order to clear the space for what we truly want and what, ultimately, will nourish us. After all, if a garden is choked with weeds and brambles, you have to dig them out and clear the space before you can plant new flowers and shrubs. In order for beautiful things to flourish, you need to clear the ground for them.

QUESTION: Is there something you need to let go of? Do you need to create the space in your life for new seeds to take root and grow?

Confusion is the state of promise,
the fertile void where surprise is possible again.
Confusion is in fact the state we are in, and we should
be wise to cultivate it.
Paul Goodman

By letting it go it all gets done;
The world is won by those who let it go.
Lao Tzu

Tip 50: Last Words

True friendship is like sound health;
the value of it is seldom known until it be lost.
Charles Caleb Colton

I've never forgotten this story which was recounted to me many years ago by a retired vicar — describing an event that had taken place at a funeral where he was officiating.

At the end of the service, as the coffin was being carried out of the church, one of the mourners jumped to his feet, ran after the coffin and grabbed onto it, crying in a highly distraught manner *"I'm so sorry. I didn't mean to say those things. Please forgive me. I didn't mean it. I'm so sorry."*

I found this image profoundly troubling. You're left wondering what on earth this person had done or said, and thinking how awful it was that now it was too late and they didn't have the chance to right the wrong they felt they had done.

Last year one of my oldest friends died — quite unexpectedly and far, far too young. I'd been thinking that I should give her a call and see how she was, maybe make a plan to get together. Now it's too late and I can't. I'm so sorry I didn't make that call.

No doubt you can see where this Tip is going. We just don't know what's going to happen and when it might be too late to say the things we need to say to someone in our life. This is particularly pertinent if there has been some kind of misunderstanding or conflict.

Is there someone you've had a disagreement or argument with and with whom you need to smooth the waters? Is there someone in your life who needs to know that you love them, or how much you appreciate them?

Please don't put it off. Don't wait until 'the time feels right' — or easier — or whatever. You just don't know when the opportunity might be taken away from you.

Ever has it been that love knows not its own depth
until the hour of separation.
Kahlil Gibran

Never part without loving words to
think of during your absence.
It may be that you will not meet again in this life.
Jean Paul Richter

Hold a true friend with both your hands.
Nigerian Proverb

Tip 51: Christmas Stress Survival Kit

I don't know the key to success,
but the key to failure is trying to please everybody.
Bill Cosby

The holiday season is upon us — the cash tills are ringing — the car parks are chocka — the shops are heaving — and stress levels are rising. Christmas is such an important event in our calendar, but over the years it seems to have become increasingly stressful, and for some the day itself is regarded with an apprehension verging on dread.

For perfectionists this time of year can be a real nightmare as the Need To Do Things Perfectly swings into overdrive. Advertising induces huge pressure to roll out the perfect Christmas: perfect gifts — perfect parties — how to cook the perfect turkey ... It's relentless.

So here are a few ideas which may help to ease the stress and allow you some space to enjoy the festive season. (I appreciate that there will be readers who don't observe or celebrate Christmas, but I hope you'll find some useful points in this tip nonetheless.)

Ask for help/support
If the majority of the work falls on your shoulders please don't suffer alone. If you do you'll have an exhausting Christmas and you're likely to end up feeling resentful. Ask for help from those around you.

Beware 'shoulds'

Christmas is full of 'shoulds'. Be hyper-aware of how often this word crops up. It almost always implies that you're about to embark on something you don't really want to do — but feel you ought to. In other words, the impetus is stemming from external expectations. The antidote is to replace the word *should* with *could*, which instantly introduces the element of choice. No, you don't have to brave the crowds to buy one more gift ... you could, but you might choose not to.

Temper expectations...

... of others and, more importantly, of yourself. Don't sweat the small stuff. Let go of being perfect — it's OK to get it wrong. This personal story from Tips reader, Carole Fossey, is a great example of getting things into perspective:

My Grandad, who we were very close to and loved immensely, died on Christmas Eve. That's the big stuff. As a result everyone really chilled out about the unimportant. We burnt the sausage and bacon rolls, the bread sauce should have been called bread lumps, we forgot a whole bag of presents under the stairs that we remembered 2 days later, but no-one cared. It just wasn't important. What was important was sharing the joy on our daughter's face and our baby's smiles as he saw the tree lights and presents. At 3pm we toasted the memory of those separated from us, and we remembered that ultimately what is important is being with those you love.

May you have a joyful and stress-free Christmas.

*I'd rather have roses on my table
than diamonds on my neck.*
Emma Goldman

*Oh, for the good old days when people would stop
Christmas shopping when they ran out of money.*
Author Unknown

Tip 52: 'Tis the Season ... for Reflection

Year's end is neither an end nor a beginning but a going on,
with all the wisdom that experience can instil in us.
Hal Borland

While everyone is frantically busy in the run-up to Christmas, the space between Christmas and the end of the year can be a great time to take a step back and reflect on the ups and downs of the past year, see what lessons there are to be learned, and to make some plans for the coming year.

For those who really want to get their teeth into this, Jinny Ditzler's book *Your Best Year Yet,* takes you through the process using ten specific steps. Here are a few to get you started.

First, make an extensive list of all you've achieved during this current year. Include absolutely everything, big or small. If you do nothing else at the end of the year I strongly recommend you do this. You'll be surprised at the number of things you have achieved and how good it feels to acknowledge them.

Secondly, consider anything that didn't go as well as you'd hoped, or things you'd intended to do but didn't. What can you learn from this? Can you take this learning into next year to ensure you don't make the same mistakes again?

Thirdly, consider what you would like your focus to be in the coming year. What will your priorities be? What's really important to you? What successes do you want to build on? Are there things in your life that you'd like to drop altogether? Is it time to make some radical changes?

Having done that, come up with a list of your Top Ten Goals for the coming year. Ditzler suggests that when pondering these goals it can help to consider all the different roles you play in your life (partner, sibling, parent, employee, employer, community member, sports team member, volunteer etc) and link your goals to these roles. Don't forget to include goals that relate to your role as 'yourself' as well ... This helps to make sure you get a good balance between work and rest.

Whatever you decide, I hope you have a wonderful Christmas and a happy, healthy and peaceful New Year.

We spend January 1 walking through our lives, room by room,
drawing up a list of work to be done, cracks to be patched.
Maybe this year, to balance the list, we ought to walk
through the rooms of our lives... not looking for flaws,
but for potential.
Ellen Goodman

Cheers to a new year and another chance
for us to get it right.
Oprah Winfrey

A Note from Annabel

I really hope you've enjoyed reading *52 Ways to Transform Your Life*. If you've been inspired by the Tips in this book and feel ready to make some changes in your life, there are a number of ways you can keep in touch.

▶ **Join the thousands of people who receive Coaching Tips just like these each month**

By becoming a subscriber to Annabel's Free Coaching Tips you will receive a Coaching Tip by email every month. You'll also be first to receive information about coaching workshops, talks and support groups.

To receive your Tips: Email annabel@annabelsutton.com and write 'Subscribe Tips' in the subject line. Or you can go to www.annabelsutton.com and subscribe there — as a bonus you'll receive the "Seven Secrets to Success" mini-course absolutely free.

▶ **Visit my Website** www.annabelsutton.com where you can find out more about Life Coaching, check out the Coaching Tips archive and download lots of free stuff.

▶ **Join Annabel's Tips Club**
Making changes on your own can be tough. Having the opportunity to get together with a regular support group — with coaching input and support from me — could make a huge difference to your success. Why not join us. Find out more at www.annabelsutton.com or contact me for more information.

► Have a FREE Coaching Consultation

If you feel you're ready to make some changes in your life, and are wondering whether working with a Life Coach could help, why not get in touch? We can schedule a free coaching consultation (by phone) where we can discuss your current situation and the kind of support you're looking for. You can ask questions and experience coaching for yourself. There's no obligation to take things further, but if you choose to do so, we can discuss how I — or one of my team — can help you.

► Keep in touch on Twitter
http://twitter.com/Annabel_Sutton/

► Connect with me on LinkedIn
http://uk.linkedin.com/in/annabelsutton

You can contact me by:

Phone: 01747 871196

Email: annabel@annabelsutton.com

Website: www.annabelsutton.com

I'd love to hear from you.

Whatever's next for you, I wish you every success.

Annabel

Books / People Mentioned

Tip 3:   Robert Middleton: www.actionplan.com/

Tip 5:   *The Artist's Way*, Julia Cameron. Published 1992 by Penguin Putnam

Tip 8:   Roger von Oech's "Creative Whack Pack"

Tip 9:   Ebookers survey published in Metro, March 14, 2005

Tip 10:   You can read the full article (and view some video that was shot of the event) at the Washington Post website: www.washingtonpost.com

Tip 13:   Marianne Williamson, *A Return To Love: Reflections on the Principles of A Course in Miracles.* Published 1992, Harper Collins

Tip 14:   Michael Neill: www.supercoach.com

Tip 15:   Positive Psychology: www.authentichappiness.sas.upenn.edu/Default.aspx

TIP 19:   Procrastination Buster Days www.annabelsutton.com/procrastination-busting.html

TIP 19:   Mark Forster: www.markforster.net

Tip 31:   Danny Wallace: www.join-me.co.uk

Tip 33: *The 4-Hour Work Week*, Timothy Ferriss. Published 2007 by Random House

Tip 34: *The Solutions Focus*, Paul Z. Jackson and Mark McKergow. Published 2002 by Nicholas Brealey International

Tip 36: The Mastery: www.themastery.com/index.htm

   Feel The Fear and Do It Anyway, Susan Jeffers. Published 1987 by Random House Books

Tip 37: Alastair Humphreys: www.alastairhumphreys.com/

Tip 45: Clean Language/Clean Change Company: www.cleanchange.co.uk

Tip 49: The Eden Project in Cornwall. www.edenproject.com

Tip 52: *Your Best Year Yet*, Jinny S Ditzler. Published 1994 by Thorsons